HOME MADE
COUNTRY WINES

Beer · Mead and Metheglin

Compiled by Dorothy Wise

Hamlyn Paperbacks

CONTENTS

© Copyright The Hamlyn Publishing Group Limited 1973
First published 1955 by Countrywise Books Limited
Revised editions 1957, 1961, 1963, 1964, 1973
Hamlyn Paperbacks edition 1978
Reprinted 1979, 1980, 1981

ISBN 0 600 34424 x

Hamlyn Paperbacks are published by
The Hamlyn Publishing Group Limited
Astronaut House, Feltham, Middlesex, England
from
Banda House, Cambridge Grove,
Hammersmith, London W6 0LE.

Printed in England by Hazell Watson & Viney Limited
Aylesbury, Bucks

Line drawings by Gay John Galsworthy

FOREWORD

Wine is a very necessary thing in most families, and it is often spoiled by mismanagement of putting together. For if you let it stand too long before you get it cold, and do not take great care to put your barm upon it in time it summer beams, and blinks in the tub, so that it makes your wine fret in the cask, etc., etc.

(from an eighteenth-century Domestic Cookery Book)

It is to help you avoid any 'mismanagement of putting together' that I have written the following pages.

Wine-making is one of the most exciting and rewarding of hobbies. Exciting because you help to create something, and rewarding because you can produce for yourself, and friends a great variety of wines, at a very low cost.

There is little need for me to write about the pleasure that a glass of good wine can give, especially when you have made it yourself. Try to cater for all tastes by making both sweet and dry wines. It has been my experience that country people like sweet wines, perhaps that is why so many country wine recipes recommend 4 lb. of sugar to the gallon.

Home wines have been made in this country from time immemorial, recipes and methods being handed down from one generation to the next. But with the advent of tea, so quick and easy to brew, the art of wine-making was almost lost.

Happily, people are once again beginning to take an interest in brewing their own wines, and several books on the subject have been published in recent years. In this little book I hope to show you how easy it is to make your own wine.

If you are a beginner, and this book is mainly for beginners, choose your recipe with care. See that you have the necessary equipment. It is recommended that you purchase fermentation jars from Boots or any wine-making equipment stockist. Treat yourself to an airlock (also called a fermentation trap). These little gadgets are not very expensive, and you can buy them complete with the cork to fit the fermentation jar.

To make things as clear as possible for you there are helpful line drawings to show how some processes in wine-making are carried out.

Do not be surprised or discouraged if your wine does not taste strongly of the fruit it is made of. Wines seldom do. Remember it is a wine that you have made, and not a cordial. If you haven't yet acquired a taste for wines, you will do so as you progress with your wine-making. Try drinking a glass of elderflower with your dinner, and see how much it improves your appetite.

DOROTHY WISE
Home-Made Wine Expert of *The Farmers Weekly*

SOME USEFUL FACTS AND FIGURES

Imperial weights and measures have been used throughout this book. When cups are mentioned in recipes they refer to the B.S.1 measuring cup which holds ½ pint or 10 fluid ounces.

When measuring flowers use a pint or quart measure and press the flowers down lightly.

METRIC WEIGHTS AND MEASURES

From the following chart you will see that 1 oz. (fl. oz.) is approximately 28 g. (ml.) but for ease of measuring it is recommended that solids and liquids should be taken to the nearest number of grammes and millilitres which can be divided by 25.

Ounces and fluid oz.	Approx. g. and ml. to nearest whole figure	Approx. to the nearest unit of 25
1	28	25
2	57	50
3	85	75
4	113	125
5	142	150
6	170	175
7	198	200
8	226	225
9	255	250
10	283	275
12	340	350
16	456	450
20	569	575

Note: When converting quantities over 20 oz. first add the appropriate figures in the column giving the nearest whole number of grammes, *not* those to the nearest unit of 25, then adjust to the nearest unit of 25.

6 tablespoons (4 fl. oz.) 125 ml.
8 tablespoons ($\frac{1}{4}$ pint) 150 ml.
$\frac{1}{2}$ pint (10 fl. oz.) 275 ml.
1 pint (20 fl. oz.) 575 ml.
1 gallon is equal to approximately $4\frac{1}{2}$ litres

TEMPERATURE CONVERSION

To convert °F to °C subtract 32, then multiply by $\frac{5}{9}$.

Notes for American users appear on the inside back cover.

WINE VOCABULARY

Airlock Fitted to the fermentation jar to protect the wine from contamination during fermentation. It excludes air but allows the carbon dioxide to escape.

Bouquet The aroma of a wine.

Campden tablets Used for sterilising the equipment.

Carbon dioxide The gas given off during fermentation.

Isinglass Can be used to clear a cloudy wine.

Lees The deposit or sediment that settles at the bottom of the jar during fermentation.

Macerate To bruise flower petals and mash fruit for the must.

Must The prepared solution before it ferments and turns into wine.

Racking Syphoning the wine off the lees. It is both necessary and beneficial to rack wines. It often helps to clear a cloudy wine.

Vinegar bacteria Airborne bacteria which can turn wine into vinegar—it must be kept out of the fermenting must at all costs.

Working or fermentation Both mean the same thing. Fermentation is the action of the yeast on the must. During this process carbon dioxide is given off and alcohol is produced. When wine is fermenting or, as some say, working, it bubbles and a slight hissing can be heard.

Yeast The fermenting agent in wine-making.

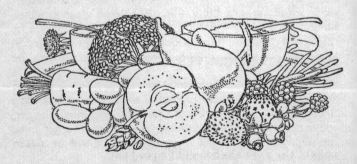

WINE-MAKING

THE FERMENTATION PROCESS

If you are going to make wine, and I hope that you are, it is just as well to have some idea what happens in the jar during the fermentation process.

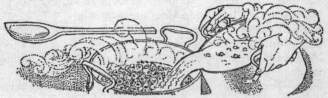

Preparing the must – boiling water being poured over the fruit in a bowl.

You prepare a lukewarm liquid (the must) that contains sugar, and other necessary ingredients, and to this you add the yeast.

Yeast is a minute plant organism, slightly oval in shape. It can multiply itself with amazing rapidity under the right circumstances. Each yeast cell buds, in order to reproduce itself, and when the bud is large enough it breaks away and commences to bud on its own account. Each cell is capable of budding anything up to thirty times before it dies.

Having added the yeast to the must, though you will not notice it for an hour or two, it will begin to feed on the sugar, and multiply and in doing so it will give off alcohol, which remains in the must, and carbon dioxide which escapes through the airlock. The airlock allows the carbon dioxide to escape without allowing air to come into contact with the fermenting must.

Not that air in itself is harmful, but the bug *mycoderma acetii* (vinegar bacteria) must be kept out at all costs. More often than not this bug is airborne. Also, by excluding the air, you eventually force the yeast to get its oxygen supply from the sugar, and the more sugar it breaks down to obtain oxygen, the more alcohol will be produced.

The yeast will go on feeding on the sugar until either the sugar supply is finished, in which case you will end up with a dry wine, unless you add more sugar, or the concentration of alcohol in the must becomes too high for the yeast to survive. Some yeasts can work to a higher alcohol content than others.

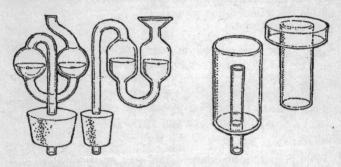

Various kinds of airlocks (fermentation locks) available.

To do its work properly yeast needs:

Warmth
Sugar
Oxygen
Acid
Nitrogenous matter (usually there is sufficient in the must but should you need to add more to boost the action of the yeast it can be bought in tablet form).

The last four are present in the right proportion in most recipes. If a fermentation 'sticks', that is, stops before it should, it may be due to the lack of any one or more of the above.

Sticking can also be due to too much sugar. A little added water will often remedy this state.

In order to thrive and multiply yeast cells need an acid solution. To provide the necessary acidity to the must you can add either lemon or orange juice or citric acid—use about ¼ oz.

ADDING THE YEAST

Do not add the yeast until the liquid you wish to ferment is lukewarm. The ideal temperature at which to ferment the must is between 65–75°F. A constantly warm kitchen or airing cupboard is ideal.

WINE YEASTS

Until Pasteur discovered the nature of yeast during the last century, wine-making was a rather hit and miss affair. The quality and the character of the wine depended on the type of wild yeast that predominated the brew. Nowadays the good strains of yeast are separated from the indifferent strains and cultivated, so that you can now buy special wine yeast, originating from the various wine districts of Europe.

For example, you can buy a champagne yeast for your elderflower wine, a sherry yeast for your orange wine, or a Pommard yeast for your plum wine. I used the latter to ferment a Victoria plum wine. You can also buy an All-purpose wine yeast and many more. These yeasts should be prepared according to the manufacturer's instructions—remember that they need to be made up 2 days before preparing the must.

There are wine-makers who will tell you that they *never* use yeast and yet produce wonderful wines. I think they are usually referring to varieties of fruit wine, where the fruit is gathered straight from the tree and made into wine almost at once. In this way the wild yeast on the fruit skins would, in all probability, be able to produce a reasonable beverage; however to be sure of a good fermentation at the onset I feel it wiser to add yeast.

HOW TO ADD THE SUGAR

It is advisable not to add all the sugar in one go and to add it in the form of a syrup so that the yeast can get to work on it immediately. If the sugar was added directly to the must it would probably not all dissolve and the undissolved sugar would weaken the yeast.

To make the sugar syrup dissolve 1 lb. granulated sugar in ½ pint boiling water; this will give you 1 pint syrup. The syrup should be added to the must half at a time—the first half at the onset and the remainder about 7–10 days later when the fermentation has begun to slow down. Always allow the syrup to cool completely before adding it to the must in the fermentation jar.

STERILISING THE EQUIPMENT

It is necessary to sterilise all utensils and equipment that is used in any of the processes during wine-making. This prevents any wild yeasts and vinegar bacteria in the air coming into contact with your wine and spoiling it.

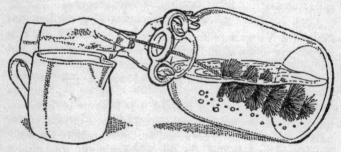

*Sterilising the fermentation jar with
Campden tablet solution.*

The best way of sterilising your equipment is to use a Campden tablet solution (crush 10 Campden tablets and dissolve in ½ pint cold water) for rinsing out the fermentation jar and other utensils. Do not wipe the equipment with a tea towel simply leave it to drain throughly on a clean surface washed down with Campden tablet solution. The prepared solution can be made to go a long way as it can be stored in a screw-topped jar and used again and again. Corks and airlocks can be sterilised by soaking them in a bowl of Campden tablet solution.

A LITTLE ADVICE ON FERMENTATION JARS

Do not fill the jar to the brim, it is both unnecessary and messy. Jars should be almost full. The handiest sized jars for a gallon of wine are those that hold a little over the gallon. If you have some must left over, ferment it in a separate bottle, keeping it well covered, and when you come to racking off for the first time, you will have some liquid for topping up with. You can also top up with cold, boiled water.

If, when your wine begins to ferment it does froth over the top of the container, insert a plug of cotton wool in the neck. When frothing subsides, remove plug, wipe the neck clean, and insert an airlock. Frothing may not occur; it depends how full your jar is and how vigorous the ferment.

Wine must be left in its fermentation jar until it has finished fermenting. You can tell when this is, by listening to it. Fermenting wine 'sings' or 'whispers' to itself. If you hear nothing, then it has finished. Also you will be able to see when it has finished working, for it will no longer bubble. So long as you can see little bubbles rising to the top, and the solution in the airlock bubbles from time to time leave it. I like to use glass fermentation jars for this very reason. Besides, the whole process is so much more interesting when you can actually see what is happening.

If your must ferments vigorously, at first, insert a cotton wool plug in the neck of the jar until the frothing subsides.

PREPARING THE AIRLOCK

To prepare the airlock for use pour in a little Campden tablet solution (1 tablet dissolved in 1 pint cold water); Insert the cork with the fermentation lock into the fermentation jar. The bottom of the stem should protrude through the cork about ½ inch and should be ½–¾ inch above the level of the must.

FIRST RACKING

Having discovered that the wine is no longer working, remove the airlock and pour off gently so as not to disturb the lees at the bottom. Or better still, syphon it off (see below), using a length of plastic tubing, a funnel, and a little muslin or filter paper to strain off any odd bits there might be floating about.

The wine should now be syphoned off into a second sterilised fermentation jar and corked firmly. Put the wine in a cool, dark place to clear. Once fermentation has completed there is no need to use an airlock. I have often left my wine in its fermentation jar for anything up to six months. Once I left 2½ gallons of elderflower wine in the jar it had fermented in for nine months before I bottled it off, and it was some of the best wine that I have ever made. But if you leave it too long, you do run the risk of off flavours developing, so generally speaking, if you rack it off after about two to three months you'll be successful.

SYPHONING

Syphoning is so much easier than pouring and does not disturb the sediment. You need about 3 feet of plastic tubing, about one-third to half an inch in diameter. Before use, sterilise it by rinsing it in Campden tablet solution. When this has been done, place one end of the tubing well down into the wine to be racked, taking care not to disturb the lees at the bottom.

Now suck gently at the other end until you get a mouthful

of wine, then pinch that end and insert it into the neck of the sterilised jar to be filled, setting this below the level of the jar being racked off. When you stop pinching the tubing, the wine will run freely into the bottle. When you want to stop the flow of wine simply pinch the end of the tube with your fingers. If you are a little nervous about syphoning have a trial run with water.

When you have racked off your wine you *may* find that its journey through the air has induced a few yeast cells to start working again, and another slight sediment will be thrown. When this has finally settled, rack the wine off again. In this way you will eventually get a stable and clear wine. Racking does a wine good, and often helps to clarify it. Finally rack your wine off into sterilised bottles and cork down.

Taste your wine as it progresses, so that you can then make any adjustments you think necessary, such as adding more syrup or lemon juice.

Maybe you will want to put a bottle of wine away to mature for some special occasion. If you do, be sure it is a wine that has been well racked. Fill the bottle so that when the cork is pushed home flush with the top the level of, the wine will be just below the bottom of the cork. Coat the top of the cork with melted paraffin wax. If you wish to lay the bottles on their sides in a rack, fill to 1½ inches below the cork and tie down.

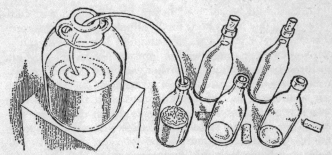

The wine being syphoned into bottles from the storage jar.

BOTTLING YOUR WINE

You will perhaps come across recipes that tell you to bottle your wine in anything from three days to three weeks. It may conceivably be ready for the storage jar in three weeks, but not in three days, or four, or five, or ten! No wine is ready for bottling at such an early date. It is not even wine at that stage!

Leave your wine to ferment to a finish, securely covered and in a warm place (about 65°F or a little warmer). By avoiding early bottling, or what amounts to fermentation in bottles, you save yourself the bother of popping corks, and I feel sure that the wine is better fermented in bulk, however small that may be, rather than in umpteen bottles.

BOTTLES AND CORKS

These must be sterilised before use with Campden tablet solution (see page 10).

By the way, I collect most of my bottles from a kind hotel proprietor, who tells me that he is glad to be rid of them. Sometimes too you will find that grocers sell vinegar, and orange squash, in useful gallon jars for fermentation.

Always use new corks. These can be bought from your supplier. Straight-sided corks are the correct ones to use, especially if you have made a quantity of wine and have several bottles to store.

Corks should be softened before use by soaking in cold water for a few hours, and finally dipping in boiling water. Drain well. A cork flogger is a useful gadget to have, but if you want to get a cork well in, and do not have a flogger, push the bottle firmly against the wall, and twist. Floggers are available from your supplier. Plastic stopper-type corks can be used for shorter storage periods, but they do not fit as tightly as the traditional ones; they do, however, have the advantage of being re-usable. A tinfoil or plastic capsule placed over the cork and a wine label on the bottle will make your wines look a little more special.

CLEARING WINES

Please do not be in too much of a hurry to clear your wines. If you have taken care in the 'putting together', and got a good ferment going, it should clear—given time. The time factor varies according to the wine. Parsnip wine often takes a long while to clear, but orange wine and certain flower wines, for example, clear fairly quickly. You must not be impatient with wine-making. Give it time, and yet more time, racking off whenever necessary. Do not forget that racking off very often helps to clear a cloudy wine, but do not mistake the cloudiness of fermentation for the cloudiness that may linger after all signs of fermentation have ceased. Someone once wrote to me complaining that their 3-month-old wine was still working, and still cloudy! You cannot expect to make wine in three months. I recently found that one batch of my parsnip wine had cleared itself, unaided, after two years. Which just goes to show what time will do!

However, if you do get a wine that will not clear even after you have given it reasonable time, you can try one of the following methods of clearing. There is nothing against drinking a cloudy wine as it is, if it is palatable, it is only the look of the thing that is against it.

THE ADDITION OF EGGSHELLS

Eggshells should be baked in a slow oven until they are brittle. Crumble them, and put a good pinch in each bottle of cloudy wine. Some old recipes include eggshells at the onset. I successfully cleared one of the few cloudy wines (a rosehip wine) I have made in this way. Into each bottle I put a good pinch of eggshell. The effect was amazing. The eggshell fragments began to sail up and down. I left the bottles alone for about a month, and when I next looked at them, the top two-thirds of each bottle was crystal clear, and the bottom third was thick and cloudy. I syphoned off the clear wine into clean bottles. It was a delicious wine.

THE ADDITION OF ISINGLASS

Here care must be taken not to add too much, because this could stabilise the cloudiness. $\frac{1}{4}$ oz. is enough to clear 10 gallons. The isinglass should be dissolved in a little warm wine. Mix this well into the bulk of the wine, then cover and leave. If your wine is already bottled, and you do not want the trouble of decanting it into a large vessel, then add a minute quantity of isinglass to each bottle. The wine should begin to clear in about 10–14 days.

With both eggshells and isinglass you must be resigned to losing a certain amount of the wine in the clearing process, because the cloudy particles sink so far, and no further. You then syphon off the clear wine into clean bottles.

THE ADDITION OF AN EGG WHITE

I have had no personal experience of clearing wine with the white of an egg. But I am told by people who have used it that it is very effective. It is said that a white of egg beaten into 1 pint of wine is sufficient to clear 15–20 gallons of wine.

ADDING SUGAR CANDY

A very old and experienced country wine-maker, who in her time thought nothing of brewing 20 gallons at one go, told me that the addition of a little sugar candy also helped to clear wines. 'A piece or two in each bottle,' she said.

I do not think, this would apply to wines that remained stubbornly cloudy after a year or so, or to wines already too sweet.

THE MALO-LACTIC FERMENT

This is a strange and exciting phenomenon that sometimes occurs during wine-making, when the tree or flower that it originated from comes into bloom. The wine, for some reason best known to itself, becomes effervescent at this time, but when the blooming is over it settles down again, and resumes normal progress.

Some people welcome this, while others deplore it. Mary Aylett in her book *Country Wines* says, 'American wine-makers call it a disease, the Swiss say no wine is really fine without it; the French say that it is of no account.' And she goes on to say, 'After reading various accounts I take the liberty of regarding the malo-lactic ferment as a gift from the gods, and will continue to bottle off my gooseberry wine when the bushes bloom in the spring'.

And this is what I do with my elderflower wine and with my gooseberry wine. So far, in spite of being racked off during the year, perhaps twice, they never fail to come to life again when their respective bushes bloom. As a result I get two delicious sparkling wines.

A friend of mine, whose approach to wine-making is wholly scientific, spoils my fun by insisting that the mysterious effervescing in my wine is due to the warm weather and nothing else!

SOME DO'S AND DON'TS OF WINE-MAKING

Do sterilise all equipment and utensils.
Do rack your wines.
Do use an airlock.
Do use wine yeasts.
Do try to keep at least one bottle of each brew back, to see what time will do.
Do use new corks.
Do keep notes and records as you go along.

Fruits and flowers for wine-making are best collected on a warm sunny day. Do not use over-ripe or over-blown ingredients.

Roots, especially parsnips, are best used after one or two frosts, when they are mature.

Above all remember that wine-making requires patience. Do not let your wine come into contact with metal at any

stage—always use plastic, glass, wooden or enamel utensils.
Do not bottle your wine too soon.

Do not use rain-wet flowers or fruit. Wait until the sun shines and dries them.

Do not attempt to bottle your wine while it is still fermenting.

Do not be in too much of a hurry to drink your wine.

Do not put fermenting wine into screw-topped bottles.

Do not allow white pith from citrus fruits to get into your brews.

Do not add all the sugar (in a syrup form) to your must all at once.

Do not sell any of your home made wines, either privately or at sales or exhibitions—it is illegal to do so.

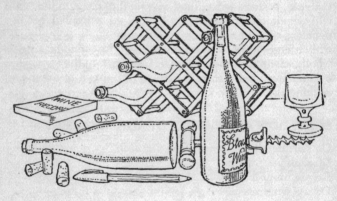

COMPETITION AND EXHIBITION

POINTS TO REMEMBER

1. Use a *plain* glass bottle and polish it until it shines.
2. Use the standard-size wine bottle (26 fluid onces).
3. Be sure that the wine to be entered or exhibited is at least a year old, and has been sufficiently racked.
4. Decant into bottle at least three days before exhibition.

5. Cork securely. A new, preferably straight-sided, cork should be used and it should be pushed in flush with the top of the bottle. If the bottle is for exhibition, the top should be painted over with paraffin wax, and a gold or silver tinfoil cap, coming a little way down the neck of the bottle, makes all the difference.
6. Label clearly with type of wine, and the *date of making*.

Judging wine—points a judge takes into account:
1. The appearance of the bottle. (Cleanliness, and the neatness and legibility of label.)
2. Clarity, and brilliance of the wine.
3. Bouquet.
4. Last but not least, the taste and texture of the wine.

Note: When you ask someone to judge wines, it is a good idea to have ready a few pieces of dry bread, and a little cheese, or a few dry plain biscuits and/or apples. I usually take my own scissors in case some of the corks are tied down and my own corkscrew, but it is just as well to provide for the unprepared judge, and have both scissors and corkscrew handy. Provide two or three clear glass wine glasses, and a bowl of warm water, and a couple of tea towels.

SERVING HOME-MADE WINES

What you serve your wines in is a matter of personal taste, but a good wine shows off to advantage in a clear thin wine glass, and I like the type that turns in slightly towards the rim. They should not be filled to the brim.

Wine decanters are attractive but I like to serve my wine out of the bottle.

Heavy-type wines, such as beetroot and elderberry, are best brought into a warm room for two or three hours before you intend to drink them. White wines, such as elderflower, or a grape wine, are best served slightly chilled but not iced. Leave them in the regrigerator (for a short time only) or a cool place until you need them.

HOME BREWED BEER AND CIDER

If you are interested in wine-making, sooner or later you will want to try your hand at brewing a gallon of beer. Here I should say that beer, legally defined, includes 'ale, porter, stout, black beer, and any other description of beer, etc.'

The history of beer goes back a long, long way into the past. The ancient Egyptians brewed beer in honour of their god Osiris, and the early Saxons drank beer at their religious festivals in worship of the gods Wotan and Thor. During the Middle Ages ale was brewed by almost every houeswife, and in the ale houses, the ale conner kept watch on the quality and the price of the ale sold. Mary Aylett recounts one of the methods used by the ale conner to detect adulteration in beer. 'Some of the beer in question was poured on to a bench, and the conner, wearing a stout pair of leather breeches, sat in it for half hour or so; if on rising his pants stuck to the seat, he knew that the beer was adulterated.' Messy but evidently effective.

TO MAKE 1 GALLON BEER YOU WILL NEED:

1 lb. malt extract	½ oz. dried hops
8 oz. granulated sugar	brewer's yeast

Heat 4 pints water and add the malt extract. Stir until dissolved. Add the sugar and stir well. Pour into a polythene bucket. Place the hops in a saucepan with 1 pint water and bring to the boil. Simmer for 10 minutes. Strain the liquid into the bucket. Repeat this with the same hops twice more. Make up to the gallon mark with cold water if necessary. When the liquid (wort) is lukewarm add the yeast according to the manufacturer's instructions. Cover and leave in a warm place. (It is advisable to stand the bucket on a tray as during fermentation the wort may froth over the top.)

Leave for 3-4 days before bottling. You will have to use your own judgment here for the brew must be still working, but only at a steady pace. The beer should be syphoned into sterilised bottles (use only proper beer or cider bottles—ordinary bottles can be very dangerous) and secured with a screw top or cap.

NETTLE BEER

2 lb. young nettles	1 lb. demerara sugar
2 lemons	1 oz. cream of tartar
1 gallon water	brewer's yeast

Use the tops of the nettles only. Put into a large saucepan with the thinly peeled rind of the lemons. Add the water and bring to the boil. Boil for 15–20 minutes. Strain on to the sugar and the cream of tartar. Stir well and when cool add the lemon juice and the yeast (prepared according to directions). Cover and leave in a warm room for 3 days. Then transfer to a cooler place for 2 days, then syphon into *strong* bottles. Cider bottles are ideal, but please do not use soft drink bottles, as they are *not* strong enough.

If the beer is still fermenting vigorously, leave the screw tops of the bottles just loose for a day before screwing down. If you use corks, do likewise, then tie down. Keep a week before drinking. This is a summer drink, *not* a wine, and it should not be kept before drinking.

CIDER

If possible let the apples weather for a time out of doors. The best way to do this is to spread them out on racks in the sun. Beat and crush the apples in a clean tub. If the quantity is small, then a stainless steel or enamelled mincer can be used. Put the pulp into a clean linen sack, or a clean hessian sack, and press out the juice. An old-fashioned wooden mangle can come in useful here. But a small fruit press is the ideal thing. Collect the juice and pour it into a fermentation jar. Fill to just below the brim and insert a cotton wool plug. Leave to stand on a tray in a warm place. It may froth over the top. If it does, wipe the neck and sides clean and renew plug. When frothing subsides insert an airlock and leave to ferment to a finish. It will be dry cider. When you want to drink it you can add 4 oz. sugar to each gallon, or more if you want it sweeter. Drink soon after adding the sugar. If you bottle off use strong bottles otherwise you run the risk of bursting bottles. I use empty cider bottles.

If you intend to make cider in large quantities I would advise you to read the subject up before you embark. The National Federation of Women's Institutes Wine Book covers the subject adequately, and so does Mrs. S. M. Tritton, in *Amateur Wine Making* (Faber and Faber).

COTTAGE CIDER

12 lb. apples	1 lb. raisins, chopped
1 gallon warm water	1½–2 lb. sugar
All-purpose yeast	

Wash the apples put them through the mincer or chop finely. Place in a polythene bucket. Add the water, raisins, sugar and previously-activated yeast. Stir well and cover. Leave in a warm place for 2 weeks stirring and pushing the pulp down daily.

Strain the liquid through two layers of muslin into a fermentation jar. Squeeze the pulp gently to extract the juice. Insert the airlock and allow to ferment right out. Transfer the jar to a cooler place for 1 month, then syphon into strong bottles and tie the corks down. This can be drunk as soon as you like but the longer you leave it the better it will be.

Note: Many people make this drink successfully without yeast.

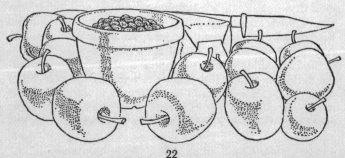

MEAD AND METHEGLIN

C. B. Dennis in his booklet, *A Background to Mead Making*, defines mead as 'the product of the vinous fermentation of honey and water, without the addition of herbs, or spices, fruit juices, or vegetable extracts'. Metheglin he calls, 'a honey-based liquor, which has been fermented, and in which spices are used'.

I do not think that you can better these two definitions.

Both drinks are of very ancient origin, and before the introduction of grapes into this country, it was usual to drink mead at festivals and at weddings. Celebrations for the latter usually lasted a full month, and this association gave rise to the word 'honeymoon'.

In wine-making the yeast gets its nourishment from various elements in the must and, as you know, in most cases acid is added in the form of lemon or orange juice.

In mead-making today, the honey used is often too pure, and if the yeast is to do its work properly, certain elements must be added. In the cruder honeys used in the old days these elements were supplied by the impurities left in.

I have used the following recipe for a yeast nutrient medium for both mead-making and wine-making. But it is most important to use it for mead-making, as it supplies just those elements missing in the honey that are essential to the vigorous growth of the yeast in the must.

FOR 1 GALLON OF MUST YOU NEED:

¼ pint water
1 tablespoon sugar
¼ teaspoon tartaric acid
mead yeast

¼ teaspoon yeast extract
¼ teaspoon ammonium phosphate

Place the water, sugar, tartaric acid and yeast extract in a pan. Bring to the boil.

Pour hot into a sterilised bottle and cover. Do this gradually, so as not to crack the bottle. When only warm add the ammonium phosphate, and shake to dissolve phosphate.

To start the mead yeast pour on some of the above nutrient when lukewarm, and place a tuft of clean cotton wool in the neck of the bottle (fill the bottle about two-thirds full). Leave to stand in a warm place (70–80°F) for 48 hours, by which time it should have a good head of froth on it. This is the time to transfer it to the must and add any remaining yeast nutrient.

When you are making more than a gallon of mead, have ready a large clean bottle holding a pint or more of the must to be fermented. Transfer your fermenting yeast starter into this bottle first, and when that too is fermenting freely, add it to the bulk of the must. An occasional gentle shake of the bottle before transfer helps the yeast, as it adds a little oxygen, also necessary to yeast at this stage.

Keep your fermenting mead well covered.

TYPE OF YEAST TO USE

Wine and mead yeasts will give the best results. I have used both a Maury and a Steinburg yeast with excellent results. Maury is said not to clear so well, but I found it cleared admirably, and produced a crystal clear mead.

If you want to save yourself a little trouble there is an extract specially prepared for fermenting honey which you will be able to purchase from your supplier.

Do not forget that if you use a wine or mead yeast, you must start it fermenting 2 days before you need to add it to the must.

WATER

Some mead-makers advocate the use of soft water, others say that this is of no importance. I would advise would-be mead-makers to try both, and judge for themselves. I have used mainly clean filtered rain water up to date.

Here then are some recipes for mead and metheglin.

DRY MEAD
(using crystalline honey)

3 lb. honey dissolved in	(if clear honey is used
enough water to	add an extra 8 oz.)
make 1 gallon	mead yeast

You will notice that I have written 'to make 1 gallon' of liquid. I have done this to make it more convenient for those of you who wish to ferment just 1 gallon of mead in a 1-gallon fermenting jar. If you add 3 lb. of honey to 1 gallon of water, you will get about $9\frac{1}{4}$ pints of liquid.

Measure and mark the level of a gallon of water in your preserving pan. Tip this water away. Now pour, or put in your honey, and add some water to dissolve the honey, and continue adding until the gallon level is reached.

Bring to the boil, and simmer for 5 minutes, no more. Then stand it aside to cool. Filter through a jelly bag, or something similar, into the fermentation jar and when lukewarm add the previously-activated yeast.

Plug the neck of the vessel with clean cotton wool, or cover with clean cotton material and leave for 2 days. When the first vigorous ferment has died down insert the airlock.

Keep in a warm temperature. Between 65–80°F is ideal. When fermentation ceases, stand vessel in a cool place for a month, and then syhpon off into clean bottles and cork.

The longer you can keep the mead the better. Some of the best meads are matured for 7 years.

SWEET MEAD
(using crystalline honey)

4 lb. honey dissolved in	(if clear honey is
water to make 1	used, add an extra 8 oz.)
gallon of liquid	mead yeast

Follow the method for dry mead, above.

If at the end of fermentation the mead is not sweet enough, add another 4 oz. honey (warmed), and stir up the contents of vessel. Replace airlock, and leave for a further three weeks.

MORE MEAD RECIPES

mead yeast	4 lb. honey
1 gallon clean rain water	1 lemon

Activate the yeast 2 days before it is required.

Boil the rain water for 5 minutes; let it cool until you just cannot bear your hand in it, or until it is about 120°F. Add the honey and stir well to dissolve. Add the lemon juice and prepared yeast. Cover and leave to ferment for 3 days then transfer to a fermentation jar and fit the airlock. When fermentation ceases move the jar to a cooler place for 1 month before bottling off.

An ancient recipe for mead, taken from an eighteenth-century recipe book reads: 'Mead. To 13 gallons of water put 30 lb. of honey; boil and scum it well; take rosemary, thyme, bay leaves and sweet briar one handful altogether; boil it an hour, put it into a tub with a little ground malt; stir it till it is lukewarm; strain it through a cloth, and put it into a tub again; cut a toast and spread it over with good yeast, and put it into the tub also; when the liquid is covered with yeast, put it in a barrel; take of cloves, mace and nutmegs, an ounce and a half; of ginger sliced an ounce; bruise the spice, tie it up in a rag, and hang it in the vessel, stopping it up close for use'.

ROSEHIP MEAD

Boil 3 lb. rosehips in 1 gallon water for 5 minutes. When cool, mash with your hands or a wooden spoon and strain through 2 layers of muslin. Make up to the gallon with boiled water if necessary. Add 4 lb. honey, and juice of 2 lemons. Stir well to dissolve honey.

When lukewarm add previously-activated yeast.

Ferment as for previous recipes.

METHEGLIN

1 sprig balm	1 lemon
1 sprig rosemary	1 gallon water
½ oz. root ginger, if liked	5 lb. honey
	mead yeast

Simmer the herbs and spices and thinly peeled lemon rind in the water for 20 minutes. Strain and pour on to the honey. Stir well to dissolve the honey. When lukewarm add the lemon juice and previously-activated yeast. Cover and leave to ferment for 24 hours. Pour into fermentation jar and insert an airlock. Leave to ferment to a finish in a warm place. Remove to a cooler place for 3 weeks before syphoning off into bottles.

Note: You can use whatever herbs you fancy. Cloves, oranges (thinly peeled rind and juice of), cinnamon, marjoram, balm, rue and hops can all be used to flavour metheglin.

27

WINE RECIPES

Where a recipe quotes 'a pint', 'a quart' or 'a gallon' of flowerheads or berries, this means sufficient to fill the measure without packing down.

All recipes marked * are by Dorothy Wise.

Before trying these recipes be sure to read the section on wine-making beginning on page 7.

APPLE WINE *

6 lb. apples, windfalls will do
1 gallon water
3 lb. sugar
1 lemon
8 oz. raisins, chopped
yeast

Wash and cut up the apples, skins, brown patches and all. Boil for 10–15 minutes in the water. Strain liquid on to the sugar and the thinly peeled rind of the lemon. Stir well. When lukewarm add the juice of the lemon, and the previously-activated yeast. Cover and leave for 24 hours in a warm place, then pour into a fermentation jar. Insert the airlock. Leave in a warm place to ferment for 4 weeks. Syphon off into a second jar, and add the chopped raisins. Insert the cork tightly and leave to mature for 6 months.

Syphon off and bottle.

APPLE AND RAISIN WINE*

6 lb. apples (if possible include 1 lb. crab apples)
1 lb. raisins
1 gallon water
3½ lb. sugar
yeast

Wash apples well and cut up. Boil with the raisins for 10-15 minutes in 1 gallon of water. Transfer everything (without straining) into a large bowl on to the sugar. Stir. When cool add the previously-activated yeast. Cover and leave to ferment for 3 days. Strain through muslin into a fermentation jar; insert the airlock. Leave to ferment to a finish in a warm place; syphon off and bottle.

APRICOT WINE*

5 lb. apricots, stoned	1 gallon water
3½ lb. sugar	yeast

Simmer the apricots until tender, then strain the liquid off on to the sugar in a large bowl. Stir well. (You can use the apricots for pies.) When lukewarm add the previously-activated yeast. Cover and leave for 24 hours. Pour into the fermentation jar; insert an airlock. Leave in a warm place to ferment to a finish. Syphon and bottle.

BARLEY WINE 1*

1 lemon	1 lb. raisins
1 orange	4 lb. demerara sugar
1 old potato	1 gallon boiling water
1 lb. pearl barley	yeast

Peel lemon and orange thinly and put peel into a large bowl. Extract the juice and put with the rinds. Scrub and slice the potato, and add to the bowl with the barley, raisins and sugar. Pour over the boiling water. Stir well. Strain into the fermentation jar and when lukewarm add the previously-activated yeast. Insert an airlock and leave to ferment in a warm place for 3–4 weeks, shaking the jar daily for the first week. When fermentation has ceased, syphon off and bottle.

BARLEY WINE 2*

1 lb. barley	1 orange
1 lb. raisins	3½ lb. white sugar
8 oz. old potatoes	1 gallon warm water
1 lemon	yeast

Put the barley, raisins, potatoes (scrubbed and sliced), thinly peeled rinds and juice of lemon and orange and sugar into a large bowl. Pour over the water, and stir well. Add the previously-activated yeast. Cover and leave to ferment in a warm place, stirring daily, for 3 weeks. Leave in a cooler place for a further week; syphon off and bottle. *Watch the corks.*

BEETROOT WINE*

6 lb. beetroot	3¼ lb. demerara sugar
1 gallon water	yeast
	1 lemon

Wash beetroot, and cut into slices. Cook gently in the water until tender. Strain and add the sugar. Stir well. When lukewarm add the previously-activated yeast and the lemon juice. Cover and leave for 24 hours in a warm place. Skim if necessary. Pour into the fermentation jar, insert an airlock and leave in a warm place to ferment to a finish. Syphon off and bottle.

SPICED BEETROOT WINE*

4 lb. beetroot	4–6 cloves
1 gallon water	½ oz. root ginger
1 lemon	3 lb. sugar
	yeast

Wash the beetroot well then slice thinly. Bring to the boil in the water with the thinly peeled rind of the lemon, cloves and ginger. Simmer until the beetroot is tender and loses its colour. Strain on to the sugar, in a large bowl. Stir well. When lukewarm add the lemon juice and previously-activated yeast. Cover and leave in a warm place, to begin fermentation, for 2 days. Then pour into the fermentation jar, insert an airlock and leave in a warm place to ferment to a finish. Syphon off and bottle.

BLACKBERRY WINE 1*

1 gallon blackberries   4 lb. loaf sugar
1 gallon boiling water   yeast

Put the berries into a large bowl and pour the water over them. Cover and leave to stand for 7 days, stirring daily. Strain through muslin on to the sugar and stir well. Add the previously-activated yeast. Transfer to the fermentation jar and insert an airlock and ferment to a finish. Syphon off and bottle.

Note: Keep this wine for at least 6 months before using.

BLACKBERRY WINE 2*

6 lb. blackberries   1 gallon boiling water
1 lemon   4 lb. sugar
yeast

Wash blackberries, peel lemon thinly and put both into a large bowl. Pour over the boiling water. Cover and let this stand for 3 days, stirring daily. Strain through muslin on to the sugar and stir well. Add the lemon juice and previously-activated yeast. Leave for 24 hours in a warm place, then pour into the fermentation jar and insert an airlock. Leave to ferment to a finish. Syphon off and bottle.

BLACKCURRANT WINE 1*

1 gallon blackcurrants 1 gallon water
4 lb. sugar

Pick the fruit on a warm sunny day. Boil the water. Let it cool to lukewarm and pour over the fruit. Cover and leave for 7 days; stir a few times. Strain off the juice on to the sugar and stir well. Pour into the fermentation jar and insert an airlock. Leave to ferment to a finish, then syphon off and bottle.

BLACKCURRANT WINE 2*

4 lb. blackcurrants   4 lb. sugar
1 gallon boiling water yeast

Remove stalks and put fruit into a large bowl. Pour over the boiling water. Stir and crush with a wooden spoon, or crush before adding the water. Cover and leave for 3 days, stirring daily. Strain through muslin, squeeze gently on to the sugar. Stir well and add the previously-activated yeast. Cover and leave to stand in a warm place to ferment. When fermentation has ceased syphon off and bottle.

BRAMBLE TIP WINE 1*

1 gallon bramble tips   3 lb. sugar
water   yeast

Gather the bramble tips when they are young. The tips should be 5–6 inches in length. Cover with cold water, and bring to the boil. Let them cool then strain. To each gallon of liquid obtained add 3 lb. sugar. Stir well, and add the previously-activated yeast. Pour into the fermentation jar and insert an airlock. Ferment to a finish, then syphon off and bottle.

Note: Keep this wine for a year before using.

BRAMBLE TIP WINE 2*

1 gallon bramble tips   3½ lb. demerara sugar
1 gallon water   or 4 lb. granulated
1 lemon or orange   sugar
              yeast

Boil the tips in the water with the thinly peeled lemon or orange rind for 30 minutes, keeping the volume of water up. Strain the liquid on to the sugar and stir well. When luke-warm add the lemon or orange juice and previously-activated yeast. Cover and leave to stand in a warm place for 24 hours, then transfer into the fermentation jar, and insert

an airlock. Ferment to a finish. Remove to a cooler place for
1 week before syphoning off and bottling.
Note: Keep this wine for 6 months before drinking.

BULLACE WINE*

1 gallon boiling water	yeast
4 lb. bullaces	1 lb. raisins, chopped
3½ lb. demerara or	
granulated sugar	

Pour the boiling water over the bullaces. When cool mash
with your hands or a wooden spoon. Stir in the sugar, and
when lukewarm add the previously-activated yeast. Cover
and leave to ferment for 3–4 days. At the end of that time
strain into the fermentation jar and add the chopped
raisins. Insert a plug of cotton wool in the neck of jar. When
fermentation subsides remove the cotton wool and insert the
airlock. Ferment to a finish. Syphon off and bottle.

BURNET WINE 1*

2 quarts burnet flowers	1 gallon boiling water
3 lb. sugar	yeast

Put flowers and sugar into a bowl and pour over the boiling
water. Stir well. When lukewarm add the previously-activated
yeast. Cover and leave to stand in a warm place to ferment for
14 days. Strain at the end of this time into the fermentation
jar. Insert an airlock, ferment to a finish. Syphon off, bottle.

BURNET WINE 2

3 quarts burnet heads	½ oz. root ginger
1 gallon water	1 lb. raisins
3 lb. sugar	2 lemons

Boil burnets and water together for 20–30 minutes; strain
the liquid on to the sugar, ginger and raisins in a bowl.

Add the thinly peeled rinds and the juice of the 2 lemons. Keep well covered, stir liquid occasionally and leave until it finishes working (about 3–6 weeks), then bottle.

Mrs. A. M. Corrie, Kirkcudbright

BURNET WINE 3*

3 quarts burnet heads	3 lb. sugar
1 lemon	8 oz. raisins
1 orange	½ oz. root ginger,
1 gallon water	optional
yeast	

Boil the burnet heads with the thinly peeled lemon and orange rind in the water for 20 minutes. Strain the liquid on to the sugar, raisins and ginger. Stir well and allow to cool. Add the lemon and orange juice and then the previously-activated yeast. Transfer to the fermentation jar and insert an airlock and leave in a warm place to ferment. Syphon off and bottle in about 3–5 weeks' time.

CARROT WINE 1*

4 lb. carrots, well scrubbed	1½ lb. granulated sugar
1 gallon boiling water	2 lemons
1½ lb. demerara sugar	2 oranges
	1 oz. root ginger
yeast	

Cook the carrots in boiling water until they are soft. Drain and add sugar to the liquid. Stir well and simmer with the thinly peeled rinds of lemons and oranges, and well-bruised ginger for a further 20 minutes. Keep liquid up to the gallon. When cool add the lemon and orange juice. Add the previously-activated yeast and let it work for 5 days, well covered. Strain into the fermentation jar, add raisins and insert an airlock. Leave to ferment to a finish in a warm place. Remove to cooler place for a few days before syphoning off and bottling.

CARROT WINE 2*

6 lb. carrots	4 oz. raisins
1 gallon water	2 oranges or 1 orange
4 lb. sugar	and 1 lemon
1 lb. wheat	yeast

Scrub carrots and cut into slices. Cover with the water, and simmer until tender. Strain liquid on to the sugar, wheat, raisins, and thinly peeled fruit rinds. When lukewarm add the previously-activated yeast and the fruit juice. Stir well, cover well and leave to ferment in a warm place for 2 weeks. Then strain into the fermentation jar and insert an airlock. Leave to ferment to a finish in a warm place. Syphon off and bottle.

Note: The longer this wine is kept the better it will be.

CARROT WINE 3

4 lb. carrots	2 lemons
1 gallon water	2 oranges
granulated sugar, see	yeast
method	

Scrub carrots until they are quite clean then with a sharp knife chop them up roughly and tie the pieces in a muslin bag. Put this with the water into a deep saucepan. When the water begins to boil lower the heat and simmer until the carrots are reduced to a soft pulp. Squeeze the contents of the bag until only dry pulp remains. Measure the whole of the liquid and to every 2 pints liquor allow 1 lb. sugar. Bring to the boil again and simmer for 30 minutes. Remove from the heat and cool. While the liquid is cooling add the grated rind and juice of the lemons and oranges. When the wine is tepid pour into the fermentation jar and add the previously-activated yeast. Insert an airlock and shake the jar every day for a fortnight. At the end of that time the wine may be strained, syphoned and bottled.

Mrs. Tarrant, Newbury, Berks

CARROT WHISKY

6 lb. carrots	4 lb. sugar
1 gallon water	12 oz. raisins, chopped
2 oranges	1 lb. clean wheat
2 lemons	yeast

Wash the carrots well (do not peel) and boil them in the water until tender. Slice the oranges and lemons and place in a bowl. Pour on the hot liquid in which the carrots were boiled. Add the sugar, stir until dissolved. Leave to stand until cool, then add the raisins, wheat and previously-activated yeast. Cover and leave to ferment for 12–15 days. Skim, syphon and bottle.

Miss R. Proctor, Luton, Beds

CELERY WINE 1*

4 lb. celery	1 orange
1 gallon water	3½ lb. sugar
2 lemons	yeast

Wash the celery and cut into short lengths. Cover with the water and bring to the boil. Add the thinly peeled lemon and orange rinds and simmer until the celery is tender. Strain on to the sugar and stir well. (The celery can be served as a vegetable if liked.) When the liquid is lukewarm, add the juice of the lemons and orange. Add the previously-activated yeast and cover and leave for 24 hours in a warm place to begin fermentation. Then pour into the fermentation jar, insert an airlock, and leave to ferment to a finish in a warm place. Syphon off and bottle.

CELERY WINE 2

Place 12 dozen sticks of washed celery in a large bowl and pour over 2 gallons boiling water and leave until the following day. Measure the liquid into a large pan and to each gallon of liquid add 3 sliced oranges and lemons and 1 oz. bruised root ginger. Bring to the boil and simmer for 5 minutes. Then pour over the sugar (4 lb. to each gallon). When nearly cold stir in the previously-activated yeast. Cover and leave in a warm place for a few days, skimming off the surface each day. Then strain into the fermentation jar, insert an airlock and leave to ferment to a finish. Syphon off and bottle.

Mrs. W. A. Shepherd, Selby, Yorks

CHERRY WINE 1*

4 lb. sweet cherries	1 gallon water
2 lb. sour cherries	4 lb. sugar
yeast	

Chop the fruit and place it in a large bowl; cover with the water. Leave for 3 days, stirring daily. Strain through two layers of butter muslin on to the sugar and heat gently stirring well, to dissolve the sugar. Remove from heat, and pour into the fermentation jar and add the previously-activated yeast. Insert an airlock, and leave in a warm place to ferment. After 3 weeks, taste. If not sweet enough add 4 oz. sugar and stir well. Leave for another week, then syphon off and bottle.

CHERRY WINE 2

cherries	pinch allspice
pinch cloves	sugar
brandy	

Stone the cherries and put them in a large jar. Place the jar in a saucepan of boiling water, cook gently until the juice is given off. Strain it through a cloth add the cloves and allspice and the same weight in sugar as juice. Boil and skim. Allow to cool, and add ½ pint brandy to each quart of syrup. Pour into bottles and cork closely.

Mrs. Trigg, Gloucester

CLOVER WINE*

3 lb. sugar	1 gallon clover
1 gallon water	blossoms, red or
2 oranges	white
2 lemons	yeast

Dissolve the sugar in the water and bring to the boil. Simmer for 5 minutes, then remove from heat and allow to cool. Peel the oranges and lemons thinly, and put the rinds into a bowl with the juice of the fruit and the flowerheads. Pour the cool liquid over and stir well. Add the previously-activated yeast cover and leave for 7 days, stirring daily. Then strain into the fermentation jar and insert an airlock. Keep in a warm place during fermentation. Syphon off and bottle at the end of fermentation.

COLTSFOOT WINE*

3½ lb. sugar	1 gallon coltsfoot
1 gallon water	flowers (they can be
2 oranges	dried and used)
2 lemons	yeast

Dissolve the sugar in the water and bring to the boil. Simmer for 5 minutes. Remove from heat and allow to cool. Peel the oranges and lemons thinly, and put the rinds into a bowl with the juice and the coltsfoot flowers (just the heads). Pour over the cooled syrup and stir. Add the previously-activated yeast, cover and leave to ferment for 7 days in a warm place. Strain into the fermentation jar and insert an airlock. When fermentation ceases syphon off and bottle.

COTTAGE BREWING

6 gallons water	2 oz. hops
2 gallons malt	1 teaspoon yeast
few twigs	

Bring half the water to the boil. Remove from the heat as soon as it boils, and let it stand till you can see your face in it. While the water is heating get ready a clean rinsing-tub with a small hole bored in the bottom and stopped up with a peg or cork. Cover it with a few birch twigs and some clean wheat straw; put a coarse bit of cloth over the bottom of the tub, then put the malt into it. Pour the water on it, and stir it well for a few minutes. Cover it close with a sack and let it stand for 3 days to keep warm near the fire, then pull out the peg or cork and let the whole run into a bucket. Put the peg in again immediately and, having prepared another 3 gallons of water (just as you did before), pour it on to the malt, and set it by the fire as before (covered close) for 2 hours. As soon as you empty the second 3 gallons of water out of the boiler put it in the first run from the malt, and boil it a $\frac{1}{4}$ hour with hops. Strain it through, and serve into a shallow vessel to cool, as quickly as possible. Run off the second 3 gallons and boil them with the same hops for $\frac{1}{2}$ hour. Strain and cool as for the first run. Mix both the runs from the malt together, add a small teaspoonful of yeast, and let it ferment for 2 or 3 days, during which time it must be frequently skimmed. 3 pints of yeast will be obtained. When fermentation is over put the beer in small cask, where it will probably ferment a little, after which stop down close.

Mrs. E. Prevett, Crawley, Sussex

COWSLIP WINE 1*

1 gallon water	6 cloves
2 quarts cowslips (just the yellow parts)	4 oranges
	2 lemons
$\frac{1}{2}$ oz. root ginger, bruised (optional)	yeast
	$4\frac{1}{4}$ lb. sugar

Pour the boiling water over the cowslips. Cover and leave for a week, stirring daily. Strain off and put 3 pints of the liquid into a saucepan with the ginger, cloves, and the thinly peeled rinds of 2 of the oranges and the lemons. Bring to the boil and simmer for 15 minutes. Make up any lost liquid with boiling water. Strain this liquid and mix it with the other liquid. Add the juice of the oranges and lemons, then the 4 lb. sugar and stir well. Lastly add the previously-activated yeast pour into the fermentation jar, insert an air-lock. Leave to ferment for 2 weeks, then add the remaining sugar and leave to ferment. When the fermentation has finished syphon off and bottle.

COWSLIP WINE 2*

4 lb. sugar	2 lemons
1 gallon water	1 gallon cowslips (just
2 oranges	the yellow parts)
	yeast

Dissolve the sugar in the water and bring to the boil. Simmer for 5 minutes, then remove from the heat and allow to cool. Peel the oranges and the lemons thinly and put the rinds into a bowl with the juice of the fruit and the yellow parts of the cowslip. Pour in the cooled liquid and stir well. Add the previously-activated yeast and leave for 5 days. Stir once a day, and keep well covered. Then strain into the fermentation jar. Insert an airlock. Keep in a warm place during fermentation. When all signs of fermentation have ceased syphon off and bottle. If the wine is dry for you, you can always add more sugar after fermentation ceases.

COWSLIP WINE 3

1 lemon	4 pints cowslip
4 pints water	flowerheads
2 lb. sugar	yeast

Peel the rind of the lemon thinly and put it in a pan with 1 pint of the water. Bring to the boil and simmer for 20 minutes. Pour over the sugar in a bowl; add the remaining water and the cowslips. Allow to cool to lukewarm then stir in the previously-activated yeast. Cover and stir every day for 3 weeks. Syphon off and bottle.

Mrs. C. A. Gilderdale, Durkar, Wakefield, Yorks

CRAB APPLE WINE*

1 gallon crab apples	3½ lb. demerara sugar
1 gallon water	8 oz. raisins
	yeast

Wash the crab apples in cold water. Slice them into a large bowl and pour the cold water over them. Cover and leave for 14 days, stirring daily. Strain through butter muslin on to the sugar and raisins, and stir to dissolve the sugar; add the previously-activated yeast. Pour into the fermentation jar, insert an airlock and leave to ferment. When fermentation ceases, move the jar to a cooler place for a few days before syphoning off the wine into bottles.

Note: Keep this wine for at least 6 months before using.

CRANBERRY WINE

1 gallon water	2 lb. raisins
1 gallon cranberries	3½ lb. sugar
	yeast

Bring the water to the boil; pour it over the cranberries in a bowl. Cover and mash daily with your hands for 6 days, squeezing all the moisture from the pulp. Add the raisins and sugar and stir until the sugar has dissolved. Add the previously-activated yeast and strain into the fermentation jar. Insert an airlock and leave to ferment for about 16 days, Syphon off and bottle.

Mrs. Baker, Barnsley, Yorks

CURRANT WINE

3 gallons water	½ pint balm
9 lb. sugar	yeast
1 gallon currants	¼ oz. isinglass

Bring the water and sugar to the boil and boil for 30 minutes, then pour over the currants. When cold add the balm and previously-activated yeast, cover and leave to ferment. When fermentation has finished add the isinglass. Pour into a barrel and leave for a month, then bottle.

Mrs. C. A. Gilderdale, Durkar, Wakefield, Yorks

DAMSON GIN 1

1 lb. damsons   12 oz. granulated sugar
1½ pints gin

Wash the damsons, halve them and remove the stones. Mix all the ingredients together and stir well until the sugar has dissolved. Store in screw-top jars in a cool, dark place for 2–3 months, shaking the jars twice a week. Syphon off the liquid into bottles, cork and store for at least a year before using.

Miss K. Cowpe, Sutton-in-Ashfield

DAMSON GIN 2

damsons   sugar
cloves   almond essence
unsweetened gin

Choose ripe damsons, wipe well and remove stalks, prick each one several times with a needle. Have ready some clean, dry quart bottles, half fill them with the fruit, shaking it well down. To each bottle add 1 clove, 2 oz. granulated sugar and a few drops of almond essence. Then fill the bottles up with unsweetened gin. Cork the bottles securely, and keep them in a moderately warm place for 3 months, shaking them occasionally. At the end of this time open the bottles and strain the gin through fine muslin until clear. Then rebottle and cork securely again and store until required.

Miss Walker, Preston, Lancs

DAMSON WINE 1*

1 gallon water	1 lemon
4 lb. damsons	1 orange
3 cloves (optional)	3 lb. sugar
yeast	

Bring half the water to the boil and pour it over the damsons in a large bowl. When cool, mash with your hands until pulpy. Add cloves and thinly peeled rinds of lemon and orange. Pour over the remaining boiling water. Cover and leave for 48 hours, stirring daily. Strain through a jelly bag or two layers of butter muslin into a pan. Add 2 lb. of the sugar and bring to the boil.

Remove from heat, allow to cool, and add the juice of the lemon and the orange. When lukewarm add the previously-activated yeast. Cover and leave for 24 hours, stirring occasionally. Pour into the fermentation jar and insert an airlock. Leave for 5 days to ferment in a warm place, then add 8 oz. sugar in syrup form (see page 9). Leave for a further 10 days before adding the next 8 oz. sugar. This wine will take up to 3 lb. sugar in all. If at the end of a further 10 days the wine is fermenting steadily, you can if you wish add a little more sugar. This feeding of the wine will result in a high alcohol content, so long as you are sure that the yeast can take it. If it cannot, you will get an oversweet wine.

I actually stopped at 3 lb. I made the wine in September, racked it into a storage jar in early February, and did not sample it until October the same year, when it was found to be a good clear, medium sweet wine.

DAMSON WINE 2*

5 lb. damsons	1 lemon
1 gallon water	4 lb. sugar
yeast	

Remove the stalks and any odd leaves. Put damsons into a bowl, and pour over half the boiling water. Let it cool, then mash with a wooden spoon or with your hands. Peel the rind of the lemon thinly and put with the pulp. Add the remaining boiling water cover and leave for 3 days, stirring each day. Strain through butter muslin, squeezing out as much juice as possible. Dissolve the sugar in the juice over low heat. Pour into a fermentation jar. Add the juice of the lemon and the previously-activated yeast. Insert an airlock. Leave in a warm place to ferment to a finish. Remove jar to a cooler place for a further week, then syphon off and bottle.

DAMSON WINE 3

Allow 1 gallon of boiling water to every 8 lb. of fruit and 2 lb. of sugar to each gallon of juice. Bruise the fruit, put it in a large bowl and pour the boiling water on it. Let it stand for 48 hours, then strain the mixture into another bowl and put in the sugar; stir until dissolved. Add the previously-activated yeast, cover and leave to ferment. When fermentation ceases syphon off and bottle; put it away in a dark place and forget it for a year.

Mrs. M. Bowden, Newton Abbot, Devon

DANDELION WINE 1*

1 gallon dandelion heads (no stalks)	3½ lb. sugar
	1 lemon
1 gallon water	1 orange
yeast	

Put the blooms in cold water and bring to the boil. Simmer for 10 minutes. Strain on to the sugar and the thinly peeled rinds of the lemon and orange. Stir well. When lukewarm add the juice of the orange, and lemon and the previously-activated yeast. Cover and leave in a warm place to begin fermentation. After 2 days, pour into the fermentation jar and insert an airlock. Leave to ferment to a finish. Remove the jar to a cooler place for a few days before syphoning off into bottles.

Note: This wine improves with keeping.

DANDELION WINE 2 (dry)*

2–3 quarts dandelion heads (with as little green as possible)	2 oranges
	2 lemons
	3 lb. white sugar
1 gallon water	yeast

Put yellow heads in a bowl. Pour over the boiling water and stir. Cover and leave for 2–3 days, stirring daily. Strain into a large preserving pan and bring to the boil with the thinly peeled rinds of the oranges and lemons. Simmer for 10 minutes, then strain on to the sugar and stir. When luke-warm transfer to the fermentation jar and add the orange and lemon juice and the previously-activated yeast. Insert an airlock and leave to ferment to a finish in a warm place. Remove the jar to a cooler place for about a week, before syphoning off and bottling.

DANDELION WINE 3 (sweet)*

3 quarts dandelion heads (no stalks)	1 lemon
	½ oz. root ginger, bruised
1 gallon water	
3½ lb. demerara sugar	8 oz. raisins
1 orange	yeast

Put the heads into a bowl. Pour over the boiling water, cover and leave for 3 days, stirring daily. Strain into a pan, add the sugar and the thinly peeled rinds of the fruit, and the root ginger. Bring to the boil and simmer for 20 minutes. Keep liquid up to original volume by adding more boiling water. Allow to cool and then strain into the fermentation jar. Add the raisins, fruit juices and previously-activated yeast. Bottle when fermentation ceases.

Note: This wine is best kept for a year before drinking.

DANDELION WINE 4

4 quarts blossoms	15 lb. sugar
4½ gallons water	6 lemons
yeast	

After washing the blossoms put them into the water, together with the sugar and thinly pared lemon rind; bring to the boil and boil for 45 minutes. Strain into an earthenware pan and leave to cool. Add lemon juice and previously-activated yeast. Pour into the fermentation jars, insert airlocks and ferment to a finish. Move the jars to a cooler place for 1 week then syphon off and bottle. Keep for at least 6 months before using.

Note: Blossoms should be picked with the sun on them.

Mrs. F. J. Keel, Near Bristol

DATE WINE*

4 lb. dates	1 orange
1 gallon water	2 lb. sugar
4 lemons	yeast

Simmer the dates for 30 minutes with the water, thinly peeled rinds of the lemons and the orange. (It improves the wine to include some of the date stones.) Strain the liquid off through two layers of butter muslin on to the sugar and stir well. When cool add the juice of the lemons and orange. Add the previously-activated yeast. Stir well and leave covered in a warm place for 24 hours. Pour into the fermentation jar and insert an airlock. Leave to ferment to a finish in a warm place. Remove the jar to a cooler place for a week before syphoning off and bottling.

ELDERBERRY PORT

2 quarts elderberries	3¼ lb. sugar
1 gallon water	4 oz. large raisins

Strip the elderberries from the stalks, add the water, bring to the boil and simmer for 15 minutes. Strain and discard the pulp. Add the sugar and raisins to the hot liquid, allow the sugar to dissolve then let the liquid cool. Ferment to a finish. Syphon off and bottle.

Note: This is a rich wine equal to port and is best kept for 1 year before drinking.

Mrs. M. Bell, Thirsk, Yorks

ELDERBERRY SYRUP

Put about 2 quarts of berries, stripped from the stalks, in a casserole in a cool oven; cover with a lid. As the juice forms keep pouring it off. Finally strain the berries through 2 layers of muslin or use a jelly bag. To each quart of juice add 1 lb. sugar and 12 cloves. Bring to the boil and simmer for 30 minutes. Strain, bottle and cork. Seal with paraffin wax.

Note: Taken in hot water this elderberry syrup is an old cure for colds.

Miss Bayley, Edinburgh

ELDERBERRY WINE 1*

4–5 lb. elderberries	6 cloves (optional)
1 gallon water	yeast, preferably a
1 lemon	Burgundy yeast
½ oz. root ginger	3½ lb. sugar
(optional)	

Strip the berries from the stalks with a fork. Put into a large bowl. Pour over the water, boiling, stir and mash with a wooden spoon. Cover and leave for 3 days, stirring daily. Strain into a pan, add the thinly peeled rind of the lemon and the spices (if used)—bruise the ginger well. Bring to the boil and simmer for 10 minutes. Allow to cool then strain over the sugar and stir well to dissolve the sugar. Add the lemon juice and lastly, when the liquid is lukewarm, add the previously-activated yeast. Pour into the fermentation jar, insert an airlock and ferment to a finish in a warm place. Syphon off and bottle.

ELDERBERRY WINE 2

1 gallon elderberries, stripped from stalks	2 gallons water
3 oz. root ginger, bruised	12 lb. lump or granulated sugar
	yeast

Put the elderberries, root ginger and water in an enamelled pan. Bring to the boil and simmer until the berries are softened. Strain the liquid on to the sugar and stir until it has dissolved. When lukewarm add the previously-activated yeast and pour into the fermentation jar. Keep back about 1 pint to fill up with as it works. Insert an airlock and ferment to a finish—it should take about 6 weeks. Syphon off and bottle.

Note: This wine can be drunk after 2 months, but the longer it is kept the better.

Mrs. Vickery, Bude, Cornwall

ELDERBERRY WINE 3

Cover the elderberries with cold water. Cover and allow to stand for 3 to 4 days, stirring and squeezing the juice several times each day. Strain and to every gallon of liquid add 3½ lb. sugar, 2 oz. bruised ginger, ½ oz. cloves and a pinch of all-spice. Bring to the boil and simmer for 30 minutes. Pour into the fermentation jar. When lukewarm add the previous-ly-activated yeast and insert an airlock. Ferment to a finish, syphon off and leave in the fermentation jar, tightly corked, for 3 months before bottling.

Mrs. Cook, Ponteland

ELDERFLOWER CHAMPAGNE

1 gallon cold water	2 lemons
1¼ lb. sugar	2 tablespoons white wine vinegar
7 heads elderflowers	

Bring the water to the boil and pour over the sugar; when cold add the flowerheads, lemon slices and the white wine vinegar. Cover and leave to stand 4–6 weeks. Syphon off and bottle, using strong bottles. Cork well as this wine is very fizzy, true to its name.

Mrs. Hall, Austwick, Lancaster

ELDERFLOWER WINE 1

9 lb. sugar	3 tablespoons lemon
3 gallons water	juice
1 egg white	yeast
½ gallon elderflowers	3 lb. plump raisins

Put the sugar, water and well beaten egg white into a pan. Bring to the boil and skim. Remove from the heat and add the elderflowers. When lukewarm add the lemon juice and previously-activated yeast. Cover and leave for 10 days, stirring well every day. Divide the raisins between 2 fermentation jars and add the liquid. Insert airlocks and bottle in 6 months' time.

Note: When well kept this wine will pass for Frontinac.

Mrs. Wilcox, Brackley, Northants

ELDERFLOWER WINE 2*

1 pint flowerlets	1 gallon boiling water
(pressed down)	3 lb. sugar
2 lemons	yeast

Put the flowerlets and the thinly peeled rinds of the lemons into a bowl. Pour the gallon of boiling water over them and stir. Cover and leave for 3 days, stirring daily. Strain on to the sugar, stir, and bring to the boil. Simmer for 10 minutes. When lukewarm pour into the fermentation jar. Add the juice of the lemons and the previously-activated yeast. Insert an airlock, and leave to ferment to a finish. Stand the jar in a cool place for a few days before syphoning off and bottling. I make this wine in June, rack it off sometime in the autumn into a fermentation jar and cork. Then I bottle it when the elderflowers bloom again, tying the corks down. You can drink it before that if you wish.

Note: I always use a champagne yeast for this wine.

FIG WINE*

2 lb. dried figs	2 oranges
3 lb. sugar	1 gallon water
2 lemons	yeast

Separate the figs and put into a bowl with the sugar and thinly peeled rinds of the lemons and oranges. Pour over the boiling water and stir well. When lukewarm add the previously-activated yeast and the juice of the lemons and oranges. Stir well. Keep in a warm place, well covered, for a week and stir once daily. Now strain through two layers of butter muslin and pour the liquid into the fermentation jar and insert an airlock. Let it remain in the warm until all signs of fermentation have ceased. Remove jar to a cool place for a week before syphoning off into bottles.

GINGER BEER

2 lemons	1 oz. cream of tartar
1½ oz. root ginger, bruised	2¼ lb. loaf sugar
	2 gallons water
½ oz. dried yeast	

Peel the lemons, squeeze and strain the juice, and put both in a bowl. Add the well-bruised ginger, the cream of tartar and sugar. Pour on the boiling water and allow to stand until just warm, then add the frothed-up yeast. Stir well together, cover with a cloth, leave in a warm place overnight. Next day skim off the yeast and bottle immediately (use strong bottles).

Note: This can be used at once, but is better if allowed to remain undisturbed for 3 days.

Miss Eirwen Jones, Merioneth

GINGER WINE 1*

2 oranges	3½ lb. demerara sugar
2 lemons	2–4 oz. root ginger
8 oz. raisins	1 gallon water
	yeast

Put the thinly peeled rinds of the fruit, the raisins, and the fruit juice in a bowl. Put the sugar, bruised ginger and water in a pan. Bring to the boil and simmer for 30 minutes, keeping the water up to the original volume. Strain on to the raisins, etc., and stir well. When lukewarm add the previously-activated yeast. Cover and leave in a warm place to ferment for 10 days. Strain into the fermentation jar and insert an airlock. Leave to ferment to a finish, then syphon off and bottle. Before bottling, taste the wine and if it is not sweet enough add a little more sugar and stir. Leave for a further week before bottling.

GINGER WINE 2

4 oz. raisins	4 oz. root ginger,
3 gallons water	bruised
9 lb. loaf sugar	4 lemons
	yeast

Stone and chop the raisins; put into a pan with water, sugar and ginger; bring to the boil and simmer for 1 hour, skimming when necessary. Pour into a tub and add the thinly pared lemon rind. When lukewarm add the previously-activated yeast. Cover and leave for 24 hours then add the strained lemon juice and pour into a cask and bung tightly. Leave for a fortnight, stirring every day. When fermentation ceases, tighten the bung. Bottle after 4 months.

Mrs. L. Wells, Kenton, Middx

GINGER WINE 3

6 lb. loaf sugar	2 gallons water
3 oz. root ginger, bruised	yeast
	½ pint brandy
8 oz. raisins, stoned and chopped	

Put the sugar, root ginger and raisins in a pan with the water. Bring to the boil and simmer for 1 hour. Strain and allow the liquid to cool to lukewarm. Add the previously-activated yeast and the brandy. Cover and leave to ferment for a fortnight. Remove any scum and put the wine into a cask. Bung lightly, leave for a week then bung closely.

Note: This wine will be ready in 2 months' time.

Mrs. A. K. Reeves, Lyminge, Kent

GOLDEN ROD WINE*

3½ lb. sugar	1 pint golden rod flowers
1 gallon water	
6 sweet oranges	yeast
8 oz. raisins, chopped	

Stir the sugar into the water, bring to the boil and simmer for 5 minutes, then pour on to the orange juice and flowers. Stir well and when lukewarm add the previously-activated yeast and leave for 5 days in a warm place, well covered, and stirring daily. Now strain off the liquid into the fermentation jar and add the chopped raisins. Insert an airlock and leave to ferment to a finish. Remove jar to a cool place for a month before syphoning off into bottles.

GOOSEBERRY WINE 1*

4 lb. ripe green gooseberries	3 lb. sugar
	1 gallon boiling water
	yeast

52

Top and tail the berries, put them in a bowl and pour over the boiling water; when softened and cool enough mash with your hands. Cover and leave for 48 hours, stirring frequently. Strain through butter muslin on to the sugar; stir well. Pour into the fermentation jar, add the previously-activated yeast and insert an airlock. Leave to ferment to a finish before syphoning off into a storage jar. Leave for 1 month before syphoning off into bottles.

Note: If possible keep this wine until the gooseberry bushes come into bloom again.

GOOSEBERRY WINE 2

Firm green gooseberries only should be used. To each 1 lb. fruit allow 2 pints cold water. To each gallon of juice obtained from the fruit allow 3 lb. loaf sugar, $\frac{1}{2}$ pint gin, $\frac{1}{4}$ oz. isinglass.

Top and tail the gooseberries, bruise them thoroughly; put in a bowl then pour over the cold water; cover and leave to stand for about 4 days, stirring frequently.

Strain through a jelly bag, dissolve the sugar in the liquid, add the gin and isinglass dissolved in a little warm water, and pour the whole into a cask; bung loosely until fermentation ceases, then tighten. Let the cask remain undisturbed for at least 6 months. At the end of that time the wine may be bottled, but it will not be ready for use for at least 12 months.

Mrs. E. Taylor, Barrow-on-Humber, Lincs

GOOSEBERRY WINE 3

To every gallon of bruised green gooseberries add 1 gallon of cold water. Cover and leave to stand for 2–3 days, stirring 2–3 times each day. To every gallon of strained liquor add 3 lb. of lump sugar and let the sugar dissolve; then put it into a barrel, and add 1 quart brandy to every 10 gallons. Leave for 6 months, then bottle.

Mrs. W. Lowe, Nottingham

GRAPE WINE 1

4 lb. grapes to each   3 lb. sugar
gallon water   ¼ oz. isinglass
¼ pint brandy

Crush the grapes and put in a bowl. Add the water to the grapes, cover and stir frequently for 3 days; strain off the liquid on to the sugar. Cover and leave for 2–3 weeks until fermentation has ceased; then dissolve the isinglass in a little warm water and add to wine, together with the brandy. Stir well. Pour into the fermentation jar, cork and leave for 6 months. Then syphon off and bottle.

Note: This wine can be drunk immediately, but is better if stored for 6 months.

Mrs. E. R. Smith, Sittingbourne, Kent

GRAPE WINE 2*

1 gallon grape juice,   1½ lb. sugar
see method   2 Campden tablets
yeast

Remove the grapes from their stalks, and crush in a large bowl with the hands. Strain through butter muslin, do not squeeze too hard. Measure the juice, and add 1½ lb. sugar to the gallon. Stir well. Dissolve the Campden tablets in a little of the juice, and add them to the bulk. Leave in a bowl for 24 hours, covered. Then syphon off into a fermentation jar and add the previously-activated yeast. Plug the neck of the jar with cotton wool. When the first violent fermentation dies down, usually in 3 days, remove plug, and insert an air-lock. Leave in a warm room to ferment to a finish. Remove the jar to a cooler place for 3 weeks, before syphoning off into a storage jar or bottles. Taste wine at this stage, and if too acid, add ¼ oz. precipitated calcium carbonate dissolved in a little of the wine. It is important to fill bottles to just below the cork, and store in a very cool place. Do not be in too much of a hurry to drink this wine; it improves with keeping. If necessary rack again into fresh bottles. Cork tightly.

Note: I would advise those interested in making wine from grapes to read *Amateur Wine Making* by S. M. Tritton, published by Faber.

GREENGAGE WINE*

4 lb. greengages	1 gallon water
3½ lb. sugar	1 lemon
yeast	

Put the fruit into a bowl with the sugar and pour over the boiling water. Add the thinly peeled rind of the lemon. When cool enough, mash with the hands. When lukewarm add the previously-activated yeast and lemon juice. Cover and keep in a warm place for a week, stirring daily. Strain into the fermentation jar and insert an airlock. Leave in a warm place to ferment to a finish. Syphon off into bottles and cork.

HAWTHORN BERRY WINE*

4 lb. berries	2 lemons
2 gallons boiling water	6 lb. brown or white
4 oranges	sugar
yeast	

Put the berries in a large bowl, and pour over the water. Cover and leave to stand for a week, stirring daily. Strain the liquid on to the thinly peeled rinds and juice of the fruit. Add the sugar and stir. Heat to lukewarm and add the previously-activated yeast. Cover and leave for 24 hours in the large bowl. Transfer to fermentation jars and insert airlocks. Leave to ferment to a finish then syphon off and bottle.

HOME MADE HOCK

2 oranges	4 lb. sugar
3 lemons	1 lb. raisins
6 medium-sized potatoes, peeled and coarsely chopped	1 gallon warm water
	yeast

Put the thinly peeled orange and lemon rind and juice in a bowl with the potatoes, sugar and raisins. Pour over the warm water and stir until the sugar has dissolved. Add the previously-activated yeast, cover and leave to ferment to a finish. Syphon off and bottle.

Mrs. Spence, Middlesborough

HOP ALE

4 oz. dried hops	6 gallons water
2 oz. dandelion root	3 lb. dark brown sugar
2 oz. gentian root (if obtainable)	3 tablespoons brewer's yeast

Boil hops, dandelion root and gentian root in the water for 2½ hours. When the liquid is almost cold, strain and add the sugar and yeast. Stir well and cover. Next day strain liquid (leaving sediment behind). Place in cask, bung tightly; leave for a few days, then it is ready for drinking.

Mr. K. Hulme, Manchester

LEMON WINE*

8–10 lemons, according to size	3½ lb. sugar or honey
1 gallon water	yeast
	8 oz. raisins (optional)

Put the thinly peeled rind of half the lemons into a pan and bring to the boil with the water. Simmer for 15 minutes. Put the lemon juice and the sugar (or honey) into a large bowl and pour over the hot liquid. Stir well. When lukewarm add the previously-activated yeast and raisins, if used. Cover and leave for 24 hours in a warm place. Pour into the fermentation jar and insert an airlock. Leave to ferment to a finish, then syphon off and bottle.

LIME BLOSSOM WINE*

3 pints lime blooms	1 lb. raisins, chopped
1 gallon water	3½ lb. sugar
1 lb. clean wheat	yeast

The blossoms from lime trees produce a wine with an exquisite flavour.

Dry the blossoms in the sun to bring out the flavour, then boil them in the water for 30 minutes. When cool add wheat, raisins and sugar; stir to dissolve the sugar. Add the previously-activated yeast, cover and leave to ferment for 3 weeks; then strain and bottle.

Note: Keep for 1 year or longer if you can before using.

LOGANBERRY WINE*

4 lb. loganberries	4 lb. sugar
1 gallon water	yeast

Put berries into a large bowl and pour over the boiling water. Mash with a wooden spoon. Cover and leave for 3 days stirring and mashing daily. Strain through 2 thicknesses of butter muslin on to the sugar and stir to dissolve the sugar. Add the previously-activated yeast. Leave in bowl covered for 24 hours then pour into the fermentation jar and insert an airlock. Keep in a warm place to ferment. Remove jar to a cooler place for 1 week then syphon off and bottle.

MALT ALE

2½ gallons malt	5 gallons water
2 oz. dried hops	3 lb. sugar
2 oz. root ginger	8 oz. brewer's yeast

Place the malt, hops and ginger in the water. Bring to the boil and simmer for 2 hours. Strain the hot liquor into a cask; add the sugar. When the liquor has cooled add the yeast. Leave for 2 days, then take off the scum and bottle the clear liquid, in strong bottles.

Mr. K. Hulme, Manchester

MANGOLD WINE 1

4 lb. mangolds	thinly peeled rind
1 gallon water	2 lemons
few pieces root ginger	juice 2 oranges
4 lb. sugar	yeast

Wash and slice the mangolds. Place in a pan with the water and bruised ginger, bring to the boil and simmer until tender. Strain into a bowl and when lukewarm strain on to the sugar, lemon rinds and orange juice. Stir to dissolve the sugar then add the previously-activated yeast. Pour into the fermentation jar, insert an airlock and ferment to a finish. Move the jar to a cooler place for 1 week before syphoning off and bottling.

Note: This wine should be made in March.

Mrs. Antell, Hucclecote, Gloucester

MANGOLD WINE 2*

4 lb. mangolds	1 gallon water
2 lemons	3½ lb. sugar
1 orange	yeast

Scrub the roots, then slice them and place in a large saucepan with the thinly peeled rinds of the lemons and orange and the water. Boil until tender. Strain on to the sugar and stir well; add the fruit juices. When lukewarm add the previously-activated yeast. Cover and leave for 24 hours in a warm place. Pour into the fermentation jar and insert an airlock. Leave in a warm place to ferment. Move the fermentation jar to a cooler place for 1 week before syphoning off and bottling.

MANGOLD WINE 3

8 lb. mangolds	4 lb. sugar
1 oz. root ginger	2 teaspoons dried hops
1 gallon water	3 oranges
	yeast

Scrub the unpeeled mangolds and slice. Place in a pan with the bruised ginger and water. Bring to the boil and simmer for 1 hour. Strain into a pan and add the sugar, hops and thinly peeled orange rind; simmer for a further 30 minutes. Allow to cool to lukewarm then add the previously-activated yeast. Cover and leave overnight. The following day, strain and add the strained orange juice, then put into a cask. Bottle in 3 months' time.

Mrs. C. W. Eden, Bedford

MARIGOLD WINE*

3 lb. sugar	2 oranges
1 gallon water	1 lemon
2 quarts marigold flowers (no green stalks)	yeast

Dissolve the sugar in the water then bring to the boil. Put the flowers, the thinly peeled rind of 1 orange, and the lemon and the fruit juice into a large bowl. Pour over the hot syrup. Allow to cool then add the previously-activated yeast. Stir well, cover and leave in a warm place to ferment for a week. Strain into the fermentation jar, insert an airlock, and leave in a warm place to ferment to a finish. Remove jar to a cooler place for 3 weeks, before syphoning off and bottling.

MARROW RUM*

1 ripe marrow	yeast
demerara sugar	1 orange

The marrow should be ripe and the skin tough and hard. Using a bread saw, cut the stalk end off and scoop out the pith and seeds. Pack the cavity with demerara sugar, pour over the previously-activated yeast and the juice of the orange. Replace the top of the marrow, and seal it well with adhesive tape. Hang the marrow, with the cut end uppermost in a muslin bag, and suspend it in a warm place. Alternatively you can stand the marrow in a tall jug or earthenware vessel and cover securely with a thick cloth. After 3 weeks the liquid inside the marrow may show signs of leaking out. When this occurs make a hole in the bottom of the marrow and allow the liquid to run out into a fermentation jar. (You see the necessity for a good tough skin.) Insert an airlock, and leave to ferment to a finish. You can if you wish add a few raisins to the liquid when you run it into the fermentation jar. Syphon off and bottle.

Note: The longer you can keep this the better it will be.

MAY BLOSSOM WINE*

1 gallon water	3½ lb. sugar
1 lemon	2 pints May blossoms
1 orange	yeast

Bring the water to the boil. Add the thinly peeled lemon and orange rinds. Add the sugar and stir with a wooden spoon to dissolve the sugar. Bring back to the boil and simmer for 15 minutes. Put the blossoms into a large bowl. Pour over the hot syrup and fruit rinds. Allow to cool to lukewarm, then add the previously-activated yeast and lemon and orange juice. Stir, cover with a cloth and leave in a warm place for 3 days, stirring daily. Strain the liquid into the fermentation jar—do not fill to the brim. Keep in a warm place; plug the neck with cotton wool for 2 days. If the must froths up, wipe the neck clean and renew the cotton wool.

When frothing subsides, remove the cotton wool and insert an airlock; ferment to a finish in a warm place. When fermentation has ceased remove the jar to a cooler place for 2 weeks, then syphon off into a storage jar or bottles and cork.

MULBERRY WINE*

4 lb. ripe mulberries	3½ lb. sugar
1 gallon water	yeast

Put the mulberries into a large bowl, and crush them with a wooden spoon. Pour the boiling water over them and stir. Add the sugar and stir well to dissolve. When lukewarm add the previously-activated yeast. Cover and leave for 4 days to ferment in a warm place. Strain through 2 thicknesses of butter muslin, and pour into the fermentation jar. Insert an airlock and leave to ferment to a finish. Remove to a cooler place for 1 week or so before bottling.
Note: Keep for a year before sampling.

OAK LEAF WINE

1 gallon boiling water	1 lemon
1 gallon oak leaves	2 oranges
4 lb. sugar	yeast

Pour the boiling water over the oak leaves and leave to stand, well covered, for 24 hours. Strain off the liquid and place in a pan with the sugar, thinly peeled lemon and orange rind and juice. Bring to the boil and simmer for 20 minutes. When lukewarm add the previously-activated yeast and strain into the fermentation jar and insert an airlock. Leave to ferment to a finish, then syphon off from the sediment. Store, tightly corked, for at least 6 months before bottling.
Note: The flavour can be varied by picking the leaves when quite young, when fully developed or even later in the year when they are beginning to turn brown. A wine may be made using walnut leaves in the same fashion.

Mrs. Potter, Leigh-on-Sea, Essex

ORANGE WINE 1*

12 sweet oranges	3¼ lb. sugar
2 lemons	6 pints cold water
1 lb. raisins, chopped	2 pints boiling water
yeast	

Wash the oranges and peel 6 of them very thinly. Put the rind in a moderately hot oven (400°F, 200°C, Gas Mark 6) to brown. Meanwhile put the orange and lemon juice in a bowl with the raisins and sugar. Pour over the water and stir well. When the rind is well browned remove it from the oven and place it in a jug and pour over the boiling water and leave to infuse for 1 hour. Then strain off the liquid and put it with the other ingredients. Add the previously-activated yeast, cover and leave in a warm place for 2–3 days stirring daily. Pour into the fermentation jar, insert an airlock and ferment to a finish. Remove jar to a cooler place after fermentation dies down, for 2 weeks. Then syphon off and bottle.

ORANGE WINE 2

6 sweet oranges	orange
2 lemons	4 lb. sugar
1 pint water to each	

Slice the oranges and lemons and place in a bowl. Pour over water, cover and leave for 5 days, stirring daily. Then strain and return the liquid to the bowl, add the sugar. Stir to dissolve the sugar, cover and allow to stand in a cool place for 3 weeks, stirring well once or twice each day. Then strain and place in a fermentation jar, cork and leave for 6 weeks. Strain again, and bottle; add 2 teaspoons whisky to each bottle.

Mrs. H. A. Measons, Uttoxeter, Staffs

PARSLEY WINE 1*

1 lb. parsley	2 oranges
½ oz. root ginger, bruised (optional)	1 gallon water
	4 lb. brown or
2 lemons	granulated sugar

yeast

Put the parsley, bruised ginger (if used) and thinly peeled lemon and orange rind in a pan with the water. Bring to the boil and simmer for 20 minutes. Strain on to the sugar and stir well to dissolve the sugar. When lukewarm add the previously-activated yeast and the fruit juice. Stir, cover and leave for 24 hours. Pour into the fermentation jar and insert an airlock. Leave in a warm place to ferment to a finish. Syphon off and bottle.

PARSLEY WINE 2

1 lb. fresh parsley	piece root ginger
10 pints water	2 lemons
3 lb. sugar	yeast

Boil the well-washed parsley in the water until tender. Strain the liquid into a bowl. Add sugar, ginger and sliced lemons. Stir well until the sugar has dissolved. When lukewarm add the previously-activated yeast, and leave lightly covered for 2 weeks. Skim off the top; then syphon off and bottle.

Mrs. M. Marsh, Trentham, Stoke-on-Trent

PARSNIP WINE 1*

4 lb. parsnips, scrubbed and sliced	1 orange
	1 gallon water
½ oz. root ginger (optional)	3 lb. sugar
	sherry or Burgundy
2 lemons	yeast

Boil the parsnip slices, the bruised ginger (if used) and the thinly peeled rinds of the lemons and orange in the water, until the parsnips are just tender. Do not over boil. Strain the liquid on to the sugar, and stir well. When lukewarm add the previously-activated yeast and the fruit juices. Leave for 24 hours, well covered, in a warm place. Pour into the fermentation jar, insert an airlock. Leave to ferment to a finish in a warm place. Remove jar to a cooler place for a week or so before syphoning off into a clean storage jar. Fill to just below cork. Leave for 6 months, then syphon off into bottles.

Variation: For sugar beet wine substitute sugar beet for parsnips.

PARSNIP WINE 2

4 lb. parsnips	8 oz. wheat
1 gallon water	1 lemon
3½ lb. sugar	8 oz. large raisins
¼ oz. root ginger	yeast

Clean the parsnips, cut them into two; put into the water and boil gently until tender. Strain, add the sugar and well-bruised ginger to the liquid. Boil for 5 minutes. Turn the liquid into a bowl, add juice and rind of the lemon and the chopped raisins. Let it cool before adding the previously-activated yeast and the wheat. Ferment for 14 days, then syphon off and bottle.

Mrs. Baker, Barnsley, Yorks

PARSNIP WINE 3

3½ lb. parsnips	2 lemons, sliced
10 pints cold water	2 lb. sugar
2 oz. root ginger	yeast
8 oz. raisins	

Wash the parsnips but do not peel. Cut them up and put into a large bowl with the cold water. Bruise the ginger and add it to the bowl with the lemon slices. Cover and leave to stand for 24 hours. Then transfer to a saucepan and cook until the parsnips are soft, but not mushy. Strain the liquid on to the sugar and stir to dissolve the sugar. Leave to cool, then add the previously-activated yeast. Cover and leave for 12 hours, then strain into the fermentation jar and add the raisins. Insert an airlock and ferment to a finish. Leave for 3 months, then syphon off and bottle.

Mrs. G. Nurse, Wytton, Hunts

PARSNIP CORDIAL

| 3 lb. parsnips, sliced | 3 lb. sugar |
| 1 gallon water | yeast |

To every gallon of water use 3 lb. of sliced parsnips. Boil them in the water until tender, then strain off the liquor Add 3 lb. of sugar to each gallon and boil again for 45 minutes. Leave to cool, and when lukewarm add the previously-activated yeast. Strain into the fermentation jar, insert an airlock and leave to ferment to a finish. Leave for 6 months before syphoning off and bottling.

Miss K. Cowpe, Sutton-in-Ashfield

PEA POD WINE 1*

4 lb. pea pods	1 gallon water
1 lemon	3½ lb. sugar
yeast	

Boil the pea pods with the thinly peeled rind of the lemon and water until tender. Strain on to the sugar and stir well to dissolve the sugar. When lukewarm add the previously-activated yeast and the juice of the lemon. Stir and leave for 24 hours in a warm place, well covered. Pour into the fermentation jar and insert an airlock. Leave to ferment to a finish in a warm place. Syphon off and bottle.
Note: This wine cleared very quickly when I made it. The longer it is kept the better it is.

PEA POD WINE 2

5 lb. pea pods	3 lb. sugar
1 gallon water	1 oz. yeast

Boil the pea pods in the water until tender; strain, then add the sugar and boil for 20 minutes. Turn into an earthenware vessel and add the previously-activated yeast. Cover and leave to ferment to a finish in a warm place, then syphon off and bottle.

Note: The longer this wine is kept the better it tastes.

Mrs. E. Harland, Goathland, Yorks

PEAR WINE*

6 ripe pears and 2 unripe or cooking pears	8 oz. raisins, chopped
	3 lb. sugar
	2 lemons
1 gallon boiling water	yeast

Wipe the pears and cut them into small chunks and place in the boiling water. Add the chopped raisins and simmer for 5 minutes. Remove from the heat and pour into a bowl. Cover and leave for 3 days, stirring daily. Strain on to the sugar and stir well to dissolve the sugar. Add the lemon juice and previously-activated yeast. Pour into the fermentation jar, insert an airlock and keep in a warm place until all signs of fermentation have ceased. Remove the jar to a cooler place for 2 weeks, before syphoning off into bottles.

PLUM WINE*

4 lb. plums	1 lemon, sliced
¼ oz. root ginger	1 gallon water
4 cloves	3 lb. sugar
yeast*	

*I have used a Pommard yeast with this recipe. It produced delicious pale-pink, medium sweet wine. Burgundy yeast itable.

Cut up the plums and remove the stones. Bruise the ginger and add to the plums with the cloves and sliced lemon. Pour over the water, boiling, and stir. Cover and leave for 3–4 days, stirring twice daily with a wooden spoon. Strain through 2 layers of butter muslin on to the sugar. Stir to dissolve the sugar and when the liquid is lukewarm add the previously-activated yeast. Pour into the fermentation jar and insert an airlock. Leave to ferment to a finish in a warm place. Syphon off into a storage jar and cork.

POTATO WINE 1

4 lb. potatoes, scrubbed and sliced	$\frac{1}{4}$ oz. hops
	1 gallon water
1 lemon, sliced	$3\frac{1}{2}$ lb. demerara sugar
yeast	

Put the potatoes, lemon, hops and water into a pan. Bring to the boil and cook until the potatoes are just soft. Strain the liquid on to the sugar. When lukewarm add the previously-activated yeast. Next day place in a barrel and cork loosely. Cork tightly when the wine has finished working. Syphon off and bottle in 3 weeks' time.

Mrs. Antell, Hucclecote, Gloucester

POTATO WINE 2

1 gallon small potatoes, scrubbed	1 orange
	3 lb. sugar
2 gallons water	few raisins
3 lemons	yeast

Cut each potato in half but do not peel them; boil in the water until just tender, but not broken, with the peel from the lemons and orange. Strain, add the sugar and the juice of the lemons and orange to the strained liquid. Bring to the boil again and when cool pour into the fermentation jar add a few raisins and previously-activated yeast. Insert an airlock and ferment to a finish in a warm place. Move the jar to a cooler place for 2 weeks before syphoning off and bottling.

Note: Leave this wine for at least 9 months before using it.

Mrs. B. Noble, Salisbury, Wilts

POTATO WINE 3*

5 lb. old potatoes	½ oz. root ginger, well bruised
1 gallon water	
2 lemons	3½ lb. demerara sugar
1 orange	yeast

Scrub the potatoes clean, and cut them into quarters. Boil them in the water for not longer than 15 minutes. Strain the liquid off on to the thinly peeled rinds of the lemons and orange and the ginger. Boil for 10 minutes, keeping the water up to 1 gallon. Pour this on to the sugar, and stir well to dissolve the sugar. When lukewarm add the fruit juices and the previously-activated yeast. Cover and leave for 24 hours in a warm place. Pour into the fermentation jar, insert an airlock and leave to ferment to a finish in a warm place. Syphon off into a storage jar, cork and leave for 3 months. Syphon off again into bottles.

Note: If liked a few raisins can be added to the wine when it is syphoned off into the storage jar.

QUINCE WINE*

20–24 quinces	3 lb. sugar
1 gallon water	2 lemons
	yeast

Wash the quinces and grate or chop finely, discarding the cores. Boil in the water for 15 minutes. Strain on to the sugar and stir well to dissolve the sugar. When lukewarm add the juice of the 2 lemons and the previously-activated yeast. ....er and allow to stand in a warm place for 24 hours. Pour ....fermentation jar and insert an airlock. Ferment to a finish in a warm place. Remove the jar to a cooler place for 2 weeks before syphoning off into bottles.

RAISIN WINE 1*

3 lb. good quality raisins	3 lb. demerara or granulated sugar
1 lemon	1 gallon lukewarm water
yeast	

Wash the raisins and remove stalks. Chop and put into the fermentation jar with the juice and thinly peeled rind of the lemon and half the sugar. Add the lukewarm water and previously-activated yeast. Insert an airlock and shake well; leave in a warm place for 10 days, shaking the jar once or twice for the first 2 days. Add the remaining sugar. Shake well to dissolve the sugar or add this in syrup form (see page 9). Ferment to a finish in a warm place. Syphon off into a storage jar, and fill it to just below the cork. Remove jar to a cooler place for 3 months before syphoning off and bottling.

RAISIN WINE 2

2 lb. raisins	1 lemon, sliced
1 pint wheat	4 lb. demerara sugar
2 large potatoes, peeled and sliced	1 gallon water
	yeast

Put raisins, wheat, potatoes, lemon and sugar in an earthenware bowl; pour on the hot, not boiling, water and when cool add the previously-activated yeast. Cover and stir each day for 21 days, then syphon off and bottle.

Mrs. Bird, Bury St. Edmunds, Suffolk

RASPBERRY WINE 1

To every quart of well-picked raspberries put a quart of water, bruise, cover and leave to stand for 2 days; strain off the liquor, and to every gallon add 3 lb. of lump sugar. When dissolved put the liquor into a barrel, and when ready, which will be in about 2 months, bottle it, and to each bottle add 1 tablespoon of brandy.

Mrs. N. Griffiths, Pwllheli

RASPBERRY WINE 2*

1 gallon boiling water	3½ lb. sugar
4 lb. raspberries	yeast

Pour the boiling water over the fruit and when lukewarm mash well with a wooden spoon or your hands. Cover and leave for 4 days, stirring daily. Strain well through butter muslin on to the sugar and stir well to dissolve the sugar. Add the previously-activated yeast. Cover and leave for 24 hours. Transfer to the fermentation jar, insert an airlock and leave in a warm place to ferment to a finish. Remove the jar to a cooler place for 2 weeks. Taste the wine and if you think it needs a little more sugar add some in a syrup form (see page 9). Insert the airlock and leave until any further fermentation has ceased. Syphon off and bottle.

REDCURRANT WINE*

4 lb. redcurrants	3½ lb. sugar
1 gallon boiling water	yeast

The above method for raspberry wine can be used or the currants can be put on to boil in the water for 20 minutes or until all juice is extracted; strain the juice on to the sugar and stir well. When lukewarm add the previously-activated yeast, cover and leave for 24 hours, then transfer to the fermentation jar. Insert an airlock and ferment to a finish in a warm place. Syphon off and bottle.

Note: This wine improves with keeping.

RHUBARB WINE 1*

5 lb. rhubarb	1 lemon
1 gallon water	3½ lb. sugar
8 oz. raisins	yeast

Put the rhubarb, washed and cut up small, into a large bowl. Pour over the cold water, cover and leave for 5 or 6 days stirring daily. Strain off through butter muslin and squeeze the pulp as dry as you can. Add the raisins, chopped, and the thinly peeled rind and juice of the lemon and the sugar. Stir well and heat to lukewarm to dissolve the sugar. Add the previously-activated yeast. Leave for 24 hours in a warm place well covered. Pour into the fermentation jar and insert an airlock. Leave to ferment to a finish in a warm place. Syphon off and bottle.

RHUBARB WINE 2

1 gallon cold water	1 oz. ground cinnamon
5 lb. rhubarb	2 lemons, sliced
3½ lb. brown sugar	yeast
isinglass	

Put the water and rhubarb, cut small but not peeled, in a bowl. Cover and leave to stand for a week, stirring daily. Then strain on to the sugar and add the cinnamon, sliced lemons and previously-activated yeast. Cover again and leave for a week, stirring daily. Strain into the fermentation jar, insert an airlock and ferment to a finish in a warm place. In about 2 months' time add some isinglass to clear the wine, then syphon off and bottle.

Mrs. E. M. Davies, Langadock, Carmarthenshire

ROSEHIP WINE*

4 lb. rosehips	1 gallon water
1 lemon	yeast, preferably a
3 lb. sugar	sherry yeast

If you can, gather the rosehips after a good frost. Wash and mince or chop the rosehips and place in a large bowl with the thinly peeled lemon rind, juice and sugar. Add the boiling water and stir well. When lukewarm add the previously-activated yeast. Cover closely and leave in a warm place for 10 days, stirring daily. Strain through 2 layers of muslin into the fermentation jar and insert an airlock. Leave to ferment to a finish in a warm place. Remove jar to a cooler place for 1 week before syphoning off into a storage jar. Leave in the storage jar, topped up and corked down for 6 months. Syphon off and bottle.

Note: You can top up the storage jar with cold, boiled water or, better still, brandy or vodka.

ROSE PETAL WINE 1*

3 lb. sugar	6 pints strong-scented
1 gallon water	rose petals
2 lemons	yeast

Dissolve the sugar in the water, add the thinly peeled rinds of the lemons and bring to the boil. Allow to cool then pour over the petals and the fruit juice. Stir well and add the previously-activated yeast. Cover well and leave to ferment, stirring daily, for 7 days. Strain off into the fermentation jar, insert an airlock and leave to ferment to a finish.

Note: I haven't made this wine myself, but a friend using this recipe produced a beautiful clear red wine.

ROSE PETAL WINE 2

4 pints rose petals	2 lb. white sugar
4 pints boiling water	yeast

This recipe for rose petal wine is a modern version of a very old recipe.

Place the rose petals in a bowl and pour over the boiling water. Leave until the water has become thoroughly impregnated with the scent of the roses then strain the liquid through muslin. Wring all the liquid out of the petals and discard them.

Place the sugar and rose liquor in a pan and bring slowly to the boil, skimming off any scum which rises; boil for 10 minutes. Allow to cool to lukewarm and add the previously-activated yeast. Pour into the fermentation jar and insert an airlock. Ferment to a finish in a warm place, then syphon off and bottle.

Note: When bottled keep the wine as long as possible as the perfume becomes richer with keeping.

Mrs. McLennan, Port Appin, Argyllshire

SLOE GIN 1

1 gallon gin	3 oz. bitter almonds
3½ lb. granulated sugar	6 pints sloes

Mix all the ingredients together and put into a 2-gallon jar. Cork and shake the jar 3 times a week. Store for 2 months, then syphon off and bottle.

Mrs. K. Cowpe, Sutton-in-Ashfield

SLOE GIN 2

Put 3 pints of ripe, dry sloes in a gallon jar with 1 oz. of sweet almonds and 1½ lb. of loaf sugar; then pour in 4 pints of gin, and cork. Shake the jar every 3 days for 3 months. Strain off the liquor, bottle and seal the corks. The gin is ready for use or may be kept for years, improving greatly in the keeping.

Mrs. Hansard, Lincoln

SLOE WINE

2 pints sloes	2 pints boiling water
1 lb. loaf sugar	

Add the boiling water to the sloes. Cover and leave to stand 4 days, stirring once or twice each day. Strain and add, to each 2 pints liquid, 1 lb. of loaf sugar. Leave for another 4 days, stirring each day. Bottle after it has well settled, but do not cork tightly until it has finished working.

Mrs. F. J. Morris, Newtown, Mont

STRAWBERRY WINE 1

10 pints strawberries   10 pints water
5 lb. sugar

Mash the strawberries and mix the pulp with the water. Mix well, cover and leave to stand overnight. The following day strain off the liquid and add the sugar; stir well until it has dissolved. Put in a barrel and bung it up for 6 months, then syphon off and bottle.

Mrs. V. E. Stewart, Moreton-in-Marsh, Glos

STRAWBERRY WINE 2*

1 gallon strawberries   3½ lb. sugar
1 gallon boiling water   8 oz. raisins
yeast

Put the strawberries into a preserving pan with the water and bring to the boil. Simmer gently until all juice is extracted, about 15–20 minutes. Strain through butter muslin on to the sugar and raisins. Stir well. When lukewarm add the previously-activated yeast. Leave for 24 hours in a warm place, well covered. Pour into the fermentation jar and insert an airlock. Ferment to a finish. Remove to a cooler place before syphoning off into a storage jar or bottles.

TEA WINE

4 pints tea   8 oz. large raisins,
2 lb. sugar   chopped
2 lemons, sliced

Pour the tea into a large bowl, add the sugar, raisins and lemon slices. Stir well, cover, and allow to stand for 4 weeks. Remove scum. Strain and put in bottles.
Note: It is then ready to use, but improves the longer it is kept.

Mrs. L. O. McMasters, Paulsgrove, Hants

VANILLA WINE

6 lb. rhubarb	2 lemons
1 gallon cold water	3½ lb. sugar
1 gallon hawthorn blossoms	

Cut up rhubarb very small. Cover with the cold water and add the hawthorn blossoms and the thinly pared lemon rind. Cover and stir daily for 2 weeks. Strain, add the sugar and stir until it is dissolved. Pour into the fermentation jar. Insert an airlock and ferment to a finish in a warm place. Syphon off into a storage jar or bottles.

Note: Leave this wine for 9 months or, better still, a year before drinking.

Mrs. McLennan, Port Appin, Argyllshire

WHEAT WINE 1*

8 oz. wheat	2 small potatoes, thinly sliced
1 lb. demerara sugar	
8 oz. granulated sugar	juice and thinly peeled rind of 2 oranges
1 lb. raisins, chopped	
4 pints cold water	yeast

Put all the ingredients into a 1-gallon jar. Add the previously-activated yeast and insert an airlock. Leave in a warm place to ferment for 3 weeks, shaking the jar daily. Syphon off and bottle.

Note: This wine can be drunk as soon as it has cleared.

WHEAT WINE 2

1 lb. wheat	4 lb. demerara sugar
1 lb. raisins, halved	1 gallon water
1 lb. potatoes, well washed and grated	yeast

Put the wheat, raisins, potatoes and sugar in a bowl together with the water. Stir in the previously-activated yeast. Cover and leave for 3 weeks, stirring every day.

Syphon off and bottle, cork tightly and keep at least 6 months before drinking.

Mrs. M. Bowden, Newton Abbot, Devon

WHEAT WINE 3

2 lb. raisins	1 gallon hot (not
4 lb. demerara sugar	boiling) water
2 pints clean wheat	yeast
juice and thinly peeled	
rind of 2 lemons	

Mix together the raisins, sugar, wheat and lemon with the hot water. When lukewarm add the previously-activated yeast, cover and leave to ferment, stirring daily, for 21 days. Then carefully strain off the liquid through a muslin cloth, do not squeeze or the wine will be cloudy. Put into bottles, and in about 4 weeks the wine will clear itself.

Note: The wine should be kept 12 months, if possible.

Mrs. E. Creasy, Woodbridge, Suffolk

A FEW ANCIENT RECIPES

Six recipes from a cookery book of the 1700's

ALMOND SHRUB

Take 3 gallons of rum or brandy, 3 quarts of orange juice, the peels of 3 lemons, 3 lb. of loaf sugar, then take 4 oz. of bitter almonds, blanch and beat them fine, mix them in 1 pint of milk, then mix them all well together. Let it stand an hour to curdle, run it through a flannel bag several times till it is clear, then bottle for use.

John Luff, Stoke Poges, Bucks

OZYAT

Blanch 1 lb. sweet almonds and the same of bitter, beat them very fine with 6 spoonfuls of orange flower water. Take 3 oz. of the cold seeds if you beat the almonds, but if you do not beat them you must take 6 oz. of the cold seeds, then with 2 quarts of spring water, rub your pounded seeds and almonds 6 times through a napkin, then add 4 lb. of treble refined sugar, boil it to a thin syrup, skim it well and when it is cold, bottle it.

John Luff, Stoke Poges, Bucks

WALNUT MEAD

To every gallon of water put 3½ lb. of honey, boil them together 45 minutes. To every gallon of liquor put 24 walnut leaves, pour your liquor boiling hot upon them, let them stand all night, then take the leaves out and put in a spoonful of yeast and let it work 2 or 3 days, then make it up and let it stand 3 months, then bottle it.

John Luff, Stoke Poges, Bucks

RAISIN WINE

Boil 10 gallons of spring water an hour; when it is milk warm, to every gallon add 6 lb. Malagar raisins, clean picked and half chopped. Stir it up together twice a day for 9 or 10 days, then run it through a hair sieve and squeeze the raisins well with your hands, and put the liquor in your barrel, bung it close up and let it stand 3 months, and then bottle it.

John Luff, Stoke Poges, Bucks

SMYRNA RAISIN WINE

To 100 of raisins put 20 gallons of water, let it stand 14 days, then put it into your cask; when it has been in 6 months add to it 1 gallon of French brandy, and when it is fine bottle it.

John Luff, Stoke Poges, Bucks

COWSLIP WINE

Boil 20 gallons of water for 15 minutes, then add 2½ lb. of loaf sugar to every gallon of water, then boil it as long as the scum rises, till it clears itself. When almost cold pour it into a tub with 1 spoonful of yeast, let it work 1 day, then put in 32 quarts of cowslip flowers and let it work 2 or 3 days, then put it all into a barrel with the parings of 12 lemons, the same of oranges. Make the juice of them into a thick syrup with 2 or 3 lb. of loaf sugar; when the wine has done working add the syrup to it, then stop-up your barrel very well and let it stand 2 or 3 months, then bottle it.

John Luff, Stoke Poges, Bucks

INDEX